BASIC HOME REPAIRS

edited by
HARRY BUTLER

Marshall Cavendish

Published by Marshall Cavendish Books Limited
58 Old Compton Street
London W1V 5PA

©Marshall Cavendish Limited 1972-1983

Most of this material was first published
by Marshall Cavendish in
All You Need to Know about Basic Home Repairs
and in the partwork
Golden Homes

First printing 1975
Second printing 1982
Third printing 1983

Printed by Dai Nippon, Hong Kong

ISBN 0 85685 086 1

INTRODUCTION

Have you ever been plunged into the darkness when a fuse blows and not known how to cope? Or has a pipe burst, leaving you in a quandary as to what to do? If so, this book has been designed with you in mind. It contains detailed instructions for dealing with many of the most common household repairs with hundreds of step-by-step diagrams.

Those little repairs that always seem to be cropping up around the home have a way of becoming bigger and more complicated unless you know precisely how to deal with them. To help you avoid some of the potential difficulties, this book gives you the necessary information to solve nagging problems and teaches you the secrets of simple and efficient home maintenance.

See the emergency procedures recommended for dealing with cistern overflows, frozen pipes, electrical failure and many more 'panic' situations. More permanent repairs, such as what you can do about damp and draughts, blocked drains, dripping taps and decoration repairs are also included. The many illustrations and diagrams can help everyone — even those with limited practical experience.

The final section of the book — DATA SHEETS — is a handy reference for household tools and equipment with helpful hints on how each tool can be used to best advantage. Illustrated in full colour, this supplementary section will provide you with a useful guide for day-to-day repairs.

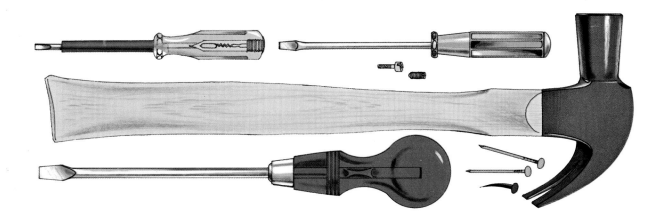

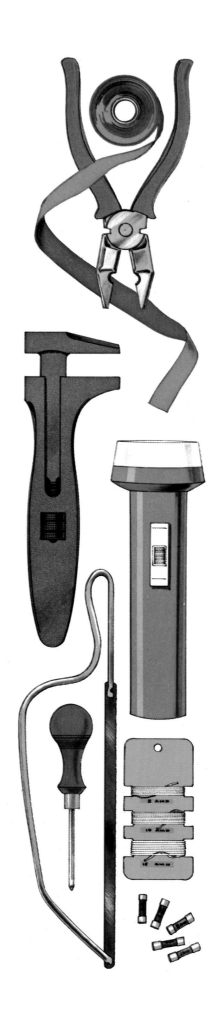

We should like to express our thanks to the
following organizations and companies for
allowing us to use their illustrations for our
drawings:
F. H. Bourner & Co. Ltd. (p. 30)
Duraflex Housecrafts Ltd. (p. 26)
Electrical Association for Women (p. 20)
Electricity Council (p. 40)
Finnish Valve Company Ltd. (pp. 29 and 31)
GKN Screws and Fasteners Ltd. (p. 53)
Grundfos Pumps Ltd. (p. 42)
Heatrae Ltd. (p. 40)
Thorn Lighting (p. 17)

CONTENTS

WHERE TROUBLES BEGIN

PLUMBING

Probably, the easiest way to understand plumbing is to start at the beginning where the clean water comes in and finish at the end where the dirty water goes out.

The pipe which carries water into your house usually has two taps. The first one is usually found in the front garden under a little metal flap. In most houses the second one is under the kitchen sink, although some older houses may have only the outside tap.

The pipe which carries water up to the cold water storage cistern at the top of the house is called *a rising main*. The cold water tap at the kitchen sink is supplied directly from the rising main before it reaches the cistern, meaning that drinking water cannot be contaminated by any dust or dirt in the cistern.

The *cistern*, meanwhile, is kept constantly full by a clever little gadget called a *ball valve*. This is a small metal or plastic ball that floats on the surface of the water at the end of a metal rod. When water is drawn from the cistern, the ball drops with the level of the water and opens the supply from the rising main. As the level of the water rises, so does the ball valve until it eventually shuts off the supply.

If anything should go wrong with this valve, an *overflow pipe*, fixed just above the level at which the ball valve should turn off the supply, prevents the cistern from overflowing into the attic. This pipe normally discharges the overflow water on to the roof or through an outside wall.

In most plumbing systems, *all the fittings*, except the cold water tap in the kitchen, are supplied from the storage cistern, although in older houses the fittings may be connected directly to the rising main. *Hot water is stored in a separate cylinder*, which is kept constantly topped up from the cistern. Normally, the water is heated by a boiler attached to the cylinder by two pipes. Since warm water has the tendency to rise, hot water is drawn up from the top of this tank and replaced with cold water at the bottom. The kitchen's cold water tap is supplied directly from the rising main.

The water supply to the *toilet* is drawn from the main cistern and is also controlled by *a ball valve* which is fitted in the small cistern attached to

PLUMBING AND WASTE SYSTEMS

1. Cold water storage cistern
2. Expansion tank
3. Expansion pipes
4. Rising main
5. Domestic stopcock
6. Company stopcock
7. Cold water supply
8. Cold water to h/w cylinder
9. Cold water to boiler
10. Boiler
11. Hot water cylinder
12. Heat exchanger
13. Hot water to cylinder
14. Return water to boiler
15. Waste pipes
16. Hopper head
17. Soil pipe
18. Vent pipe
19. Gulley trap
20. Manhole inspection chamber
21. Rain-water soakaway
22. Rain-water pipe
23. Overflow pipes
24. Drinking water
25. Hot water supply
26. Pipe to soil water sewer

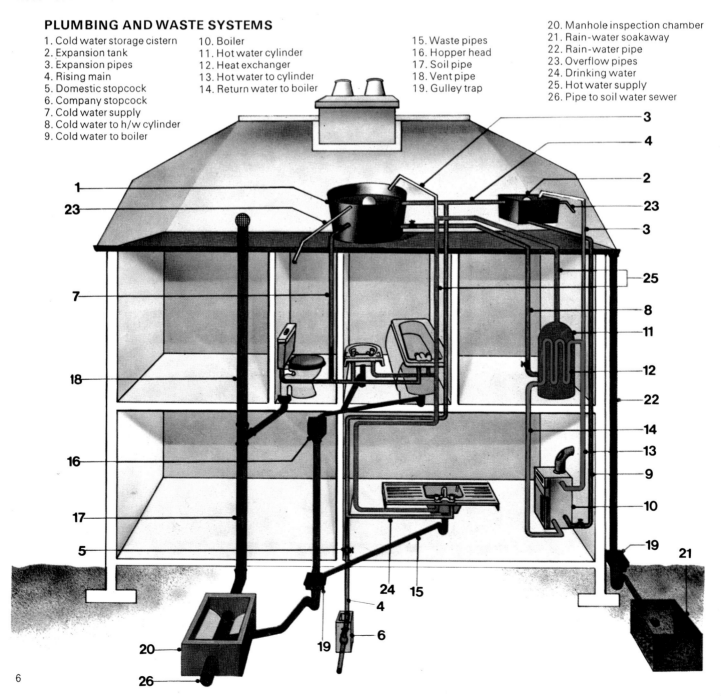

**Conventional house construction —
this is a composite of several
different types of structures.**

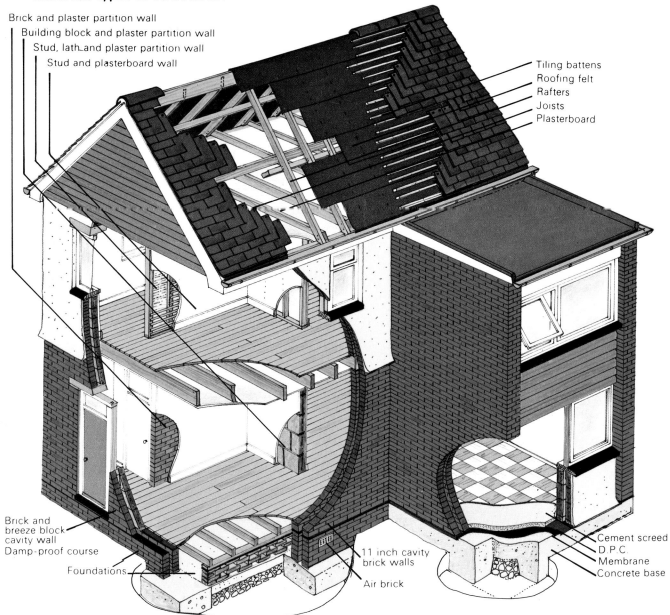

Brick and plaster partition wall
Building block and plaster partition wall
Stud, lath and plaster partition wall
Stud and plasterboard wall

Tiling battens
Roofing felt
Rafters
Joists
Plasterboard

Brick and
breeze block
cavity wall
Damp-proof course
Foundations

11 inch cavity
brick walls
Air brick

Cement screed
D.P.C.
Membrane
Concrete base

the lavatory pan. There is also an overflow pipe in case the valve goes wrong; in this case the pipe passes through the nearest exterior wall. *All other fittings*—baths, hand basins, sinks — have built-in overflow outlets which discharge directly into the waste pipes.

In order *to prevent smells from entering the house* through the drain pipes *all waste pipes have U-shaped bends in them,* close to the fitting, which trap a certain amount of water and effectively seal off smells.

The waste water which is passed out of the house through these waste pipes is fed into a single wide pipe, normally fixed to an exterior wall at the rear of the house and connected to ground-level drains.

Most *ground-level drains* have at least *two manholes* covering 'inspection chambers' at some point

before they connect with the main sewer line. You may feel, however, that 'inspecting' the drains is someone else's job. For ways and means on how to cope with plumbing problems including freeze ups, overflows and blockages, see pages 27-34.

WHAT A HOUSE IS MADE OF

Despite the infinite number of designs, the great majority of houses are built of basically the same materials put together in basically the same way.

All houses are built on *foundations* sunk into the ground. Unless there is unexpected subsidence under the house (which is rare) you will seldom, if ever, be bothered by problems with the foundations.

The most probable cause of trouble in the structure, is *the damp-proof course* — or lack of it. A damp-proof course (often called a dpc)

should seal the entire house from damp penetrating into it from the ground on which it is built. In brick houses it is normally fixed into the walls just above ground level and can be made of any strong, waterproof material, such as slate, bitumen, or lead. In timber houses it is fixed between the lowest timbers and the concrete or bricks on which they rest.

If you have concrete floors on the ground floor of your house, they will have been laid on a thick polythene sheet connected at every wall to the dpc. Without this membrane, damp would rise up through the floor because it is in direct contact with the ground. Wooden floors are always fixed just above the dpc so that no damp can get into the timber.

Although most new houses *must* have an efficient damp-proof course built into them, earlier constructions were built according to less fussy regulations. Few houses built before 1900 will have any kind of protection from damp included in the structure.

There are probably *three different types of walls* in your house. The *exterior walls* will have a cavity in the middle to improve insulation and stop damp from penetrating through the brickwork.

All *interior walls* are either *load-bearing*, meaning that they are part of the structural framework of the house and carry the weight of walls and floors directly above, or *non-load bearing*, meaning that they are simply partitions which can be removed without having any effect on the main structure. There are no easy rules to tell which are which.

Interior walls are normally built of *stud partitioning*, bricks or building blocks. Stud partitioning is a thick wooden framework onto which the plaster is fixed. Building blocks are bigger, lighter and usually cheaper than conventional bricks; they are not unlike a giant version of toy building blocks.

On solid walls of bricks or blocks, *the plaster* is applied directly to the wall. On a stud wall, it is usual in modern constructions for plasterboard ('a sandwich' of plaster between sheets of cardboard) to be nailed to the framework and then covered with a thin 'skim' of final plaster. In old houses, laths (thins strips of wood) were nailed to the studs and then plaster was applied onto the laths, but this method is rarely used now.

It is useful to know what the walls of your house are made of, if only to avoid problems when you want to hang a picture or put up a shelf (see pages 49–51). To find out whether a wall is solid or a stud partition, simply rap it with your knuckle. A stud wall has a definite hollow sound.

Floors and ceilings are fixed to thick lengths of wood called *joists*. These are normally spaced at 16 inch (407 mm) centres and are set inside the walls on each side of the room. Floorboards are nailed on top of the joists (and across them so that the joists run one way and the floorboards the other) and plasterboard is nailed under the joists to form ceilings.

If the *roof space* in your house is not used, it is unlikely that there will be any floorboards covering the joists. If you have to get up there for any reason, take great care to *step only on the joists*—the plasterboard nailed underneath will not stand much weight, and if you step on it, you will put your foot straight through the ceiling below, causing an unnecessary problem.

RADIAL WIRING
IN OLDER HOUSES

1. Company fuse and mains service cable
2. Company meter
3. Main fused switch
4. Lighting circuit fuses
5. Immersion heater fuse
6. Power circuit fuses
7. Cooker fuses
8. Round pin socket outlet
9. Cooker power switch
10. Hot water cylinder

RING MAIN WIRING

1. 2 x 5A lighting circuits
2. 15A immersion heater circuit
3. 2 x 30A ring main
4. Fused spur to bathroom heater
5. Consumer unit – mains switch
6. Company meter
7. Company fuse and mains service cable
8. 30A cooker circuit
9. Fused spur to kitchen fan
10. Hot water cylinder

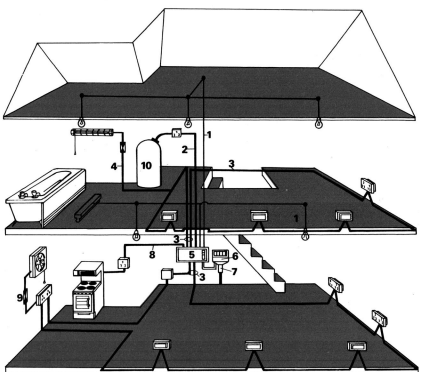

ELECTRICITY—
terms and equipment

Whether your electricity supply enters the house underground or through an overhead cable, the first item of equipment to be installed in the house is a *sealed fuse unit*. It should *never* be opened, except by the electricity board, and is the first of a number of electrical safety devices. In case of a serious fault or overload, this unit permits the electricity board to isolate your supply from that of the public.

Electricity passes through this unit via a cable containing both a *live* and a *neutral* wire. Usually an outer metal sheath provides the *earthing* point.

Fuses

Electricity is potentially a very dangerous force, and, therefore, must have safety signals attached to its flow at regular intervals. We know these safety signals as *fuses;* a fuse is simply a piece of wire which melts and breaks the circuit if too much electricity is passed through it. If you were to dangerously 'overload' the entire circuit in your home—i.e. try to use more electricity than the wiring was safely capable of carrying—then the fuse in the sealed unit would 'blow'. It would also blow if something went seriously wrong with the wiring.

The total amount of electricity that the wiring in your home can safely carry varies from area to area. Ask your local electricity authority for further information.

Switches are used in 'circuit breaker' fuse boxes.

Meters

The next piece of equipment on a domestic electricity supply is the meter, which simply records how much power you use so that your local electricity board will know how much to charge for it. Somewhere near the meter you will find the mains switch(es) which enable you to turn off the electric current to your home.

Domestic fuses

After the main cable passes through the meter, it branches into several sub-circuits which operate throughout the house. These sub-circuits are each controlled by a domestic-type fuse which can be repaired by the householder. Such fuses normally can be found in one or more fuse boxes near the meter.

Ring main wiring

The types of fuses used in your house and the number of fuse boxes depends largely on how your house is wired. In some countries, such as Great Britain, all power circuits in houses built after 1947 have been wired on what is called the *ring main* principle. This simply means that a single loop of cable runs around the house linking all the power and socket outlets; it starts and finishes at the fusebox. Depending upon the size of your house, you may have more than one ring main. It often happens that one ring controls the *ground* floor sockets and another controls the *first* floor. Furthermore, lighting and any powerful equipment such as cookers are on separate circuits.

The advantage of the ring main system is that it allows extra sockets to be installed easily and cheaply. Also all sockets and plugs are the same size. Every appliance has a small cartridge fuse in its plug. Ideally, if something goes wrong with an appliance, the entire electricity supply is not affected, the cartridge fuse blows first.

Separate cable system

In another type of system, many pre-1947 houses are wired with separate cables which lead from the meter to individual power points. This is known as *radial wiring*. Since there must be as many fuses as there are sockets, separate cable systems usually have a fuse box for all sockets, and separate fuse boxes for lighting and powerful equipment. Each box has its own mains switch.

Some of the older systems may have two fuses per circuit. If so they should be modified by the electricity board to meet modern safety standards.

It is easy to tell with which system your house is wired. If you have square pin sockets, you have a ring main system. (Actually the pins are not square, but rectangular). If you have round pin sockets, either with two or three holes, you have separate cable wiring.

Whichever system applies to your home, the first principle of safety when dealing with electricity is always this: never attempt any repairs without first turning off the mains supply—the switches are always next to the meter.

For more information about electricity, see pages 11-21.

No one should attempt to drive a car without knowing how to stop it or steer it. In the same way, no one should live in a house without knowing where the vital controls are, what they do and when to use them.

WATER SUPPLY

If you need to turn off the water, which tap do you turn and where do you find it? The most important tap, and often the most difficult one to find if you are in a hurry, is the *stop tap* which can cut off the water supply to your entire house.

Normally, this tap can be found in the front garden, under a small metal flap, and about three feet under the ground. In older houses the flap is apt to be overgrown with grass and weeds, completely hidden. If you have trouble finding it, the position of a neighbour's will probably give you an indication as to where to concentrate the search. If all else fails, the water board should be able to tell you where it is.

Finding it, however, is not necessarily the end of the problem. The tap may be set too deep in the ground for you to reach it with your hands. If so, you will need a special turn key to open it. Such a key is only a little claw on the end of a pole which enables inaccessible taps to be turned off and on. You can buy them quite cheaply in old-fashioned ironmongers, and they can save you a great deal of frustration. There is not much point knowing where the tap is if, in an emergency, you cannot reach it.

Except in some older houses, there should also be another tap on the *rising main*, inside the house. You can find this one by following the pipe leading from the cold water tap at the kitchen sink. Often it is directly underneath the sink, or in bungalows the most likely place for it to be is in the airing cupboard.

Turning off the water supply at the rising main means that no further water will enter the storage cistern on the roof and that the cold water tap in the kitchen will not work. It does not mean, however, that a burst pipe will suddenly stop spouting water — it must empty the cistern before it will do that, or the supply from the cistern must be shut off.

Most plumbing layouts have *a tap on the pipe that leads from the cistern*. It may be right next to the cistern in the attic (and often, therefore, fairly inaccessible), or it may be in the airing cupboard next to the hot water cylinder. If you cannot find either of these taps, the simplest way of emptying the cistern quickly is to turn on all the taps throughout the house and keep flushing the toilet. Remember, if you have to empty your water system, *always switch off the boiler or immersion heater.*

ELECTRICITY
If you need to turn off the electricity, do you know where the switches are? Depending upon the wiring system in your house, there may be more than one *mains switch.* If, for example, you have electric heating which stores up power during off-peak hours, you will have a special mains switch controlling that circuit alone.

Mains switches are always fixed next to, or very close to, the electricity meters, and the meters are usually fitted under the stairs or in out of the way kitchen cupboards.

Whatever you are doing with electricity, even if it is only changing a bulb, it is safest to TURN OFF ALL THE MAINS SWITCHES before you start. For this reason it is best to ensure that the meters or switches are always accessible and that you do not have to empty an entire cupboard to get at them.

Whenever you shut off your electricity supply, check any instructions for your *central heating system* or your *boiler* before turning the supply back on.

For how to replace fuses, change plugs, etc., see pages 11-21.

Words of warning
In some countries it is illegal to tamper with electricity for any reason, whether to make minor repairs or change plugs, unless you are a qualified electrician. Always check with your local electricity board before taking any action.

GAS
If you want to turn off the gas, you should find the gas supply tap next to the meter. It is usually a small lever attached to the pipe — turn it as far as it will go to cut off the supply.

Remember, when you switch the supply back on, that pilot lights in cookers and water heaters will have to be re-lit (see page 22). Do not be alarmed if they take a few minutes to light, as the gas must travel completely around the pipes again.

Even the keenest do-it-yourself fanatics are advised against tampering with gas equipment. If it is not working properly, call the gas board. And if you can smell gas and think you may have a leak, they will arrive in an amazingly short time.

EVERY HOME'S TOOL KIT
There are some tools no home should be without, even if the occupants claim they do not know one end of a hammer from the other. The simplest, most straightforward domestic maintenance jobs, the kind that crop up every day, are made far more difficult if there are no tools of any kind available. For example, it is very difficult to change a plug if you have to use the end of a knife as a screwdriver The right tool, however, will save much pain and many nicked fingers!

If you have the tools, then be sure you can find them when you want them. Keep tools together, somewhere easily accessible to you but not to the children, and put them back in the same place after you have used them. Every home needs:

Electrical screwdriver. Essential for changing plugs, replacing fuses, etc. The handle is insulated to guard against shocks. Ordinary screwdrivers will not work for most electrical jobs —

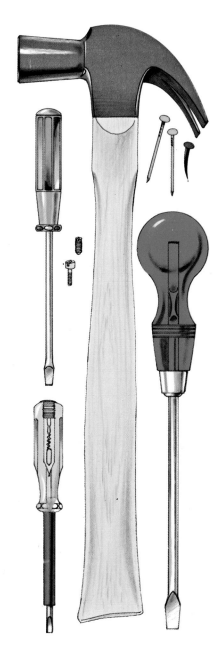

BASIC TOOLS

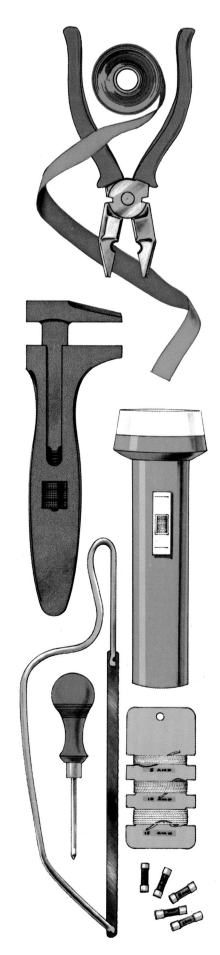

BASIC TOOLS

the blade is too thick to fit the slot of the tiny screws in most appliances.

Some special types of electrical screwdrivers have signals fixed in their handles which will flash a warning if you come in contact with a loose connection or a live wire. They are insulated to prevent you from getting a shock.

Ordinary screwdriver. Wonderfully versatile tool, but resist the temptation to use it for stirring paint and levering lids off tins. If the blade is distorted or blunted, the screwdriver is virtually useless.

Hammer. Choose a medium weight, preferably a claw type. The V-shaped notch on the other side of the hammering bit gets nails out easily if they are not completely sunk in.

Pliers. Invaluable for getting a tight grip on anything small, straightening things that are bent or bending things that are straight. Get a pair with cutting edges on the inside and you will be able to snip through cable wire without ruining the kitchen scissors.

Adjustable spanner. You may not need to undo a nut very often, but when you do you will not be able to manage without this tool. Invaluable for mending children's bicycles and mechanical toys.

Insulation tape. A precautionary material for electrical repairs. Very useful for making temporary repairs for all sorts of things from garden hoses to vacuum cleaner hoses and even punctured water pipes.

Fuse wire/fuses. Make sure you have the right thicknesses of wire to mend any fuse. Normally, it's 5, 10 and 15 amps, but look for instructions on your fuseboxes to see if you have any peculiar ones. Spare fuse cartridges that fit into 13-amp plugs will only be needed if your house is wired with a ring main.

Small metal saw. This is the cheapest, handiest saw on the market (you can get it at any local handyman's shop). It will cut through cable, small metal pipes and small pieces of wood — just about anything, in fact.

Bradawl. Useful for making holes in things, particularly holes for screws. If you make a little hole with a bradawl before putting the screw in, it will help to ensure that the screw goes in at the right place and it will be much easier to drive the screw home.

Torch. When a fuse blows and the lights go out and you cannot find a thing anywhere, make sure you can find a torch.

Right: The old and new colour-coded electric flex. The colours were changed to match the present European standard system. Only 'flex' is affected—cable, used for permanent wiring, retains the old colours.

ELECTRICITY- HOW IT WORKS

Words of warning
Please note that the discussion of *electrical equipment and repairs* applies specifically to *Great Britain*. Those persons living in other areas must contact their local electricity authority for advice before undertaking *any* repairs. In some countries, any tampering with electricity, except by a qualified electrician is *illegal*. See page 21 for Safety Precautions.

What it is
Electricity is a form of natural energy which can be generated by passing a magnet rapidly back and forth through a coil of wire. To modern man the discovery of this process means that energy can be converted to electrical power, with its ease of distribution, and then reconverted into yet other forms of energy, such as heat and light.

Voltage
Electric current flows along wires in much the same way as water flows along pipes, but it will only flow if the wire circuit is completed. At least two wires must be connected to an appliance to make a complete circuit

— a *live* wire and a *neutral* wire. If the pressure at the generating source is high, the electricity flows quickly and steadily through the circuit; if it is low, it flows more slowly. This pressure is measured in *volts*. In most parts of Britain the standard pressure, or voltage, is 240V, and electrical equipment on sale there is designed to work best at that pressure. Most appliances have a little metal label attached to them which gives their voltage.

N.B. Electrical voltages vary from country to country, and sometimes even within a country. It is essential, therefore, that all appliances be checked first to see that the voltage for which they were designed operates in your area. A higher voltage than that called for may cause the appliance to burn out.

Amperes
Another vital statistic of electricity applies to the wires through which the electricity flows. Going back to the analogy of the water supply, a very narrow pipe allows less water to flow through it than a wide pipe. So it is in electricity — a thick cable can carry more electricity than a thin wire and the amount of electric current passed is measured in amperes.

Sockets
In pre-1945 houses in Britain, which normally have a separate cable or 'radial' wiring system (see pages 8-9), you are apt to find that some sockets will be rated for *15 amps*, some for *5 amps* and some for only *2 amps*. It is important to know which is which because attempting to plug

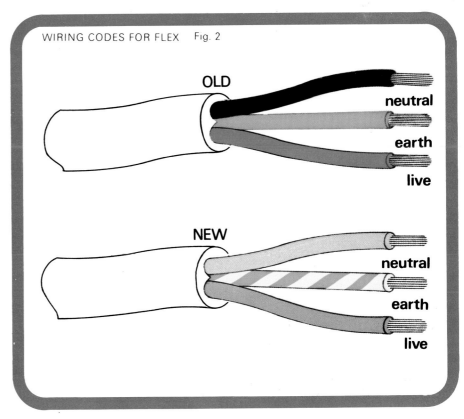

WIRING CODES FOR FLEX   Fig. 2

OLD

neutral

earth

live

NEW

neutral

earth

live

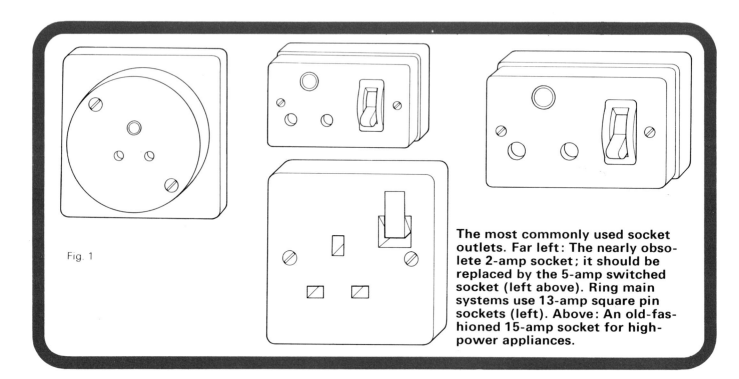

Fig. 1

The most commonly used socket outlets. Far left: The nearly obsolete 2-amp socket; it should be replaced by the 5-amp switched socket (left above). Ring main systems use 13-amp square pin sockets (left). Above: An old-fashioned 15-amp socket for high-power appliances.

an appliance requiring a lot of electricity into a socket wired to carry only a little can be very dangerous.

Modern ring main systems (see pages 8-9) have one size socket outlets throughout the home. These are *rated for 13 amps* and they *all take the same size* and *type of plug*. Fig. 1. illustrates the various types of sockets. When a choice is available, use a *socket with* its own *switch.*

To conform with modern safety regulations, *all two-pin sockets* should be *changed to three-pin* earthed sockets by a *qualified electrician.*

Watts

Finally, electrical work power is measured in *watts.* This term applies to the electrical equipment itself and is a means of measuring the *rate* at which electricity is used. An average electric light bulb uses only about 100 watts; whereas, a powerful electric fire might easily use 3,000 watts, or 3 kilowatts (there are 1,000 watts in a kilowatt — kW for short). Once you know the number of watts or kilowatts an appliance requires and its necessary voltage you can find the correct socket and flex with the appropriate amount of amperes to use.

To find out how much electricity a piece of equipment uses, multiply its wattage by the number of hours it is in use. A 300 watt appliance used for 5 hours will consume one-and-a-half chargeable units (the unit being the *kilowatt hour* — 1000 watt hours equals 1kW hour).

House wiring

The cables which carry electricity around your house from the fuse unit (see page 9) are made up of at least two and usually three separate wires— each with its own distinctive covering,

all held snugly together by an outer cover made of an insulating material such as plastic or rubber.

The *live wire* carries the electricity from the Electricity Board's generator to your home; *the neutral* wire carries it back again; and *the earth* wire is the safety wire which carries electricity to the earth if a fault should occur in the circuit.

Often, cables in a 'separate cable' system have no earth wire, but instead, are encased in a metal pipe which acts as 'an earth continuity connection, *non-metal* pipes cannot be used.

The term cable is used to refer to those wiring systems which are *fairly permanent circuits;* usually they are composed of quite stiff conductors. The thicker the conductor (usually copper wire), the greater the current that can be carried. Fairly powerful appliances (i.e. fires, washing machines) need 15 amp cable, cookers 25-50 amp, and lighting circuits 5 amp cable.

Flex (flexible cable) consists of the same wiring components (live, neutral, earth) as standard cable, but it has been specially designed to connect portable appliances to plugs and sockets. *Do not* use standard cable to connect portable equipment.

The *earth wire* is a special precaution which has been included to ensure safety. All new wiring systems include earth wires, and it is most important that they are properly connected. Should a live wire become disconnected from its proper circuit and touch a conducting material, such as the metal edge of an appliance, it is liable to cause a severe shock in anyone who touches the appliance — unless an earth wire is attached. If it is, the electricity will follow the path of least resistance to the ground and

flow through the earth instead of the person's body; at the same time the fuse will 'blow' disconnecting the supply from the faulty appliance.

Some appliances have been specially made to have only a two-core flex and no earth wire. These are known as 'double insulated' appliances and their wiring has been so well insulated that there is very little possibility of getting a shock from them. Most vacuum cleaners, hairdryers and DIY drills are in this category.

It is easy to distinguish flex wires by the colour of their coverings, which have now been standardized throughout Europe. Fig. 2 (p. 11) shows both the European standard wiring and the older British wire coding still found in older appliances and in cable.

What flex to use for what

Occasionally, you may need to change the flex on an appliance; this is especially important to do if a wire has frayed or is otherwise damaged. Most household appliances use three-core flex, which includes an earth wire for safety. In houses with a 'radial' wiring system, two-core flex may still be used with two-pin plugs to fit low-amperage sockets. However, it is advisable to have any two-pin sockets or plugs changed to three-pin ones wherever possible to conform with modern safety regulations. Your electricity authority will give help and information. One exception will be for *double-insulated* equipment, which needs only two-core flex.

3 amp two-core flex is suitable for lamps, radios, televisions and electric blankets. The *live* and *neutral wires are not identified* by colour — it does not matter which is connected to the terminals in a two pin plug, but do have two-pin plugs changed where possible. This flex can carry a 'load' of up to 720 watts.

6 amp two-core flex does have the live and neutral wires identified, and therefore should be wired correctly with the right wires fixed to the right terminals in the plug. It can carry a load of up to 1440 watts and is used for lighting and non-earthed appliances.

6 amp three-core flex is the most widely used in the home. It carries a load of up to 1440 watts and is used for refrigerators, single-bar electric fires, most small kitchen appliances, vacuum cleaners, etc.

10 amp three-core flex is used for electric kettles, two-bar radiant fires, 2 kW fan heaters, etc. It takes a load of up to 2400 watts.

15 amp three-core flex takes a load of up to 3600 watts and is used for big electric fires, washing machines, dishwashers and most of the big kitchen appliances.

45 amp heavy duty three-core cable is rarely needed in the home except for electric cookers. It carries up to 6000 watts.

Changing a plug

Although there are only four basic types of plugs in general use in Great Britain, there are actually dozens of different design variations because each manufacturer produces his own.

Some of these gentlemen ought to be informed of the error of their ways; they contrive to produce plugs of an appalling design which are unbelievably difficult to change. What should be a simple two-minute job is thus changed into an infuriating wrestle with screws, washers and other little bits of metal. When purchasing plugs, do compare designs to find those easiest to fit.

Whatever the design and whatever the size of the plug, there are a few basic similarities. On the pin side of most plugs you will find a number of screws. The two small screws near the opening for the flex are there to hold the flex secure so that it cannot be pulled out. Do not bother with these for the moment. The remaining screw is the one that holds the two parts of the plug together. Unscrew this to get at the works. (You may find that two-pin plugs have no visible screws at all. But if you hold the pins you can twist off the top casing and slide it down the flex to get at the terminals.)

Inside, the wires are invariably attached to the terminals by screws. They will either be wrapped around the screw and held underneath a washer, or they will be fitted into little holes with a screw through the top holding them in. Loosen these screws with an electrical screwdriver to remove the wires from the terminals. Then, loosen the two small screws on the pin side to release the clamp which holds the flex in the plug. Remove the flex.

If the new flex to be attached to the plug has been cut clean through, you will need to bare the wires. Beginning about two inches (50 mm) from the end of the piece use a sharp knife or a flex stripper to cut away the outer covering of the flex *only*. Take great care that you do not cut through the wire. Pull off the little insulation

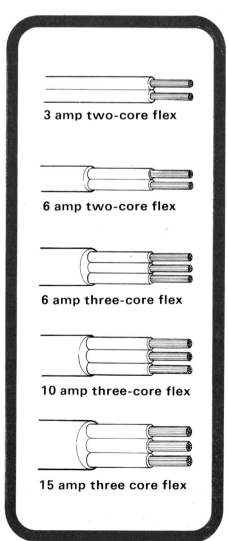

3 amp two-core flex

6 amp two-core flex

6 amp three-core flex

10 amp three-core flex

15 amp three core flex

Flexes (Key)

Neutral (N) : blue
Earth (E) : green/yellow
Live (L) : brown

Right: Connecting a 13-amp plug. 1. Remove the cover by loosening the large screw(s) on the pin side. Two metal clips hold the cartridge fuse. 2. With some plugs the flex must be inserted through the cover before connecting the wires. 3. Remove the terminal screws and a small screw holding the flex clamp. Bend the bared wires into loops. 4. Connect the wires to the proper terminals; fix them securely by tightening the terminal screws. Replace the flex clamp and screw the cover back on.

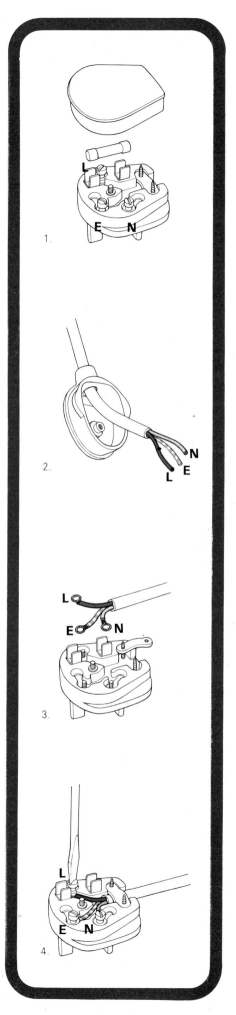

1.

2.

3.

4.

sleeves so that the wires are bared at the tips.

Now look at the cover of the plug. If there is a complete circle where the flex goes through, the cover has to be slipped over the flex before you connect it up. If each part of the plug has a semi-circle opening, the cover can be fixed on last.

Push the flex under the securing clamp far enough so that when it is tightened the clamp will be over the outer covering of the cable.

The terminals inside the plug will be marked 'L' for live (or 'R' for red in older plugs); 'N' for neutral (or 'B' for black); and 'E' for earth. It is *essential* that the right wires are connected to the right terminals, except when you are connecting two-core flex of the same colour to a two-pin plug — then it does not matter which wire is attached to which terminal.

Remember, green/yellow (or green) goes to 'E'; brown (or red) goes to 'L'; blue (or black) goes to 'N'.

In ring main circuits all plugs have the same design and are rated for 13 amps. Each plug has its own small cartridge fuse inside the plug. You will find it easier with these to connect up the *Live wire* if you unclip the cartridge.

If the terminal fixings are washers held down by screws, wrap the wire clockwise around the screw and underneath the washer so that when you tighten the screw it pulls the wire further around instead of pushing it out.

If the fixings are little holes with screws through the top, loosen the screws as far as you can without taking them out and bend the ends of the wires back double before pushing them into the holes. Always make sure there are *no loose strands of wire* sticking out anywhere.

When all the wires are securely fixed to the terminals, tighten the screws holding the cable clamp and replace the cover.

Adaptors

If you want to connect more than one plug into a socket, you can use an adaptor. You must not, of course, plug in more equipment than the circuit can carry — 15 amps on a 5 amp socket is an overload which will blow the fuse, or may cause a fire.

Other types of adaptors also allow you to connect different types of plugs into sockets, i.e. a 5 amp plug into a 15 amp socket. If *plugs are not fused*, be sure that the adaptor is; *any time* you use a plug of a *lower* amperage than the socket can carry, you *should* also lower the amperage of the *fuse*, to protect the circuit.

Adaptors for lamps must not be used to connect other appliances to sockets, as there is no earth connection in this type of adaptor.

COPING WITH FUSES

Fuses in boxes

A fuse is simply a piece of wire which can only stand so much electricity being passed through it. Every electrical circuit is 'protected' by a fuse which is designed to melt instantly — and break the circuit — if too much current goes through it. For example, a 3kW fire draws current at the rate of $12\frac{1}{2}$ amps. If it were plugged into a circuit with only 5-amp wiring, too much power would be drawn through the wires; the fuse would then melt, and break the circuit.

Fuses also 'blow' if an appliance develops a short circuit — that is, a live wire touches a neutral wire before it reaches the appliance and shortens the circuit around which the electricity would normally pass. If this happens, extra heavy current flows through the wiring and blows the fuse.

It is vitally important that every fuse is fitted with the right thickness of wire. If it is too thick, then it will not melt quickly enough to prevent trouble, and if it is too thin, then it will melt before it should. In the first case it is too dangerous and in the second it is maddening, so always make sure, when you mend a fuse, that you are using the right wire.

Why fuses blow

The first thing to remember is that there is always a reason why a fuse blows. If it is because an appliance is short circuiting, the fuse will blow as soon as you try to switch the appliance on. There is little point in mending the fuse and then trying to use the same appliance again because the fuse will only blow again.

The moral is: switch off and unplug the appliance that has caused the fuse to blow. Do not try to use it again until it has been repaired.

If the fuse has blown because of overloading — that is, when too many appliances are plugged into a single

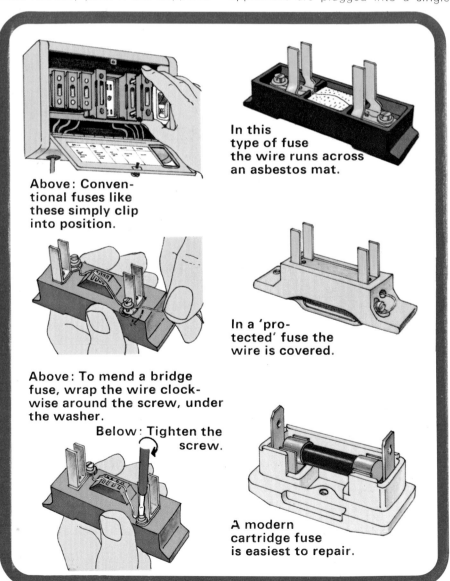

Above: Conventional fuses like these simply clip into position.

Above: To mend a bridge fuse, wrap the wire clockwise around the screw, under the washer.

Below: Tighten the screw.

In this type of fuse the wire runs across an asbestos mat.

In a 'protected' fuse the wire is covered.

A modern cartridge fuse is easiest to repair.

circuit — you should reduce the 'load' (by unplugging some) before mending the fuse. And then, do not plug in more appliances than the particular circuit can carry.

How to mend a fuse

Fuse boxes are always located next to the mains switches. Depending upon how your home is wired (ring main or radial) you may have as many as three or four separate fuse boxes and a corresponding number of mains switches. *Always turn off all the mains switches before touching any fuse.*

Most fuse boxes are covered by a plate either clipped on or held in place with a screw. When the plate is removed, you will see a neat line of fuses, all of which you will have to check. They pull out and push in quite simply.

The rating of fuse wire is always printed on the card around which it is wrapped when you buy it. Most fuse cards have lengths of 5 amp, 15 amp and 30 amp wire. The ratings of fuses are normally marked on the fuse box or moulded into the porcelain fuse holder. Some fuses are colour coded on the outside — a little white spot signifies 5 amps, a blue spot 15 amps, and red 30 amps.

Three different types of fuses are used in Britain. The most common is held in diagonally opposite corners by a screw at each end. Halfway between the screws the wire crosses a little hump, or 'bridge'. It is easy to see if the fuse has blown — the wire will have melted and you can probably notice black scorch marks around it.

To mend the fuse, loosen both screws and remove the pieces of melted wire. Cut a new length of wire, making sure it is the same amperage rating, wrap an end around one of the screws in a clockwise direction so that it does not become loose when you tighten the screw. When you have fixed it on one side, twist the other end clockwise around the second screw and tighten that. Do not make the wire too taut or it may break.

Protected fuses are also normally made of porcelain, but with this type it is more difficult to see if the wire is blown, because it is poked through a hole running lengthways through the porcelain with an exposed screw securing it at each end. To check this kind of fuse you must try to prise the wire out with a screwdriver. Obviously, if it is blown, it will slip out easily.

You mend a protected fuse in exactly the same way as a bridge fuse. Loosen both screws, remove the old wire, fix one end of the new wire first, then poke it through the hole until it comes out on the other side and twist it around the second screw.

Cartridge fuses do not have bare wire at all; instead, the fuse is encased in an insulated cylinder with a metal cap at each end. To mend this kind of

fuse you simply unclip the entire cartridge and clip in a replacement with the same rating.

Although they are simpler and neater than conventional fuses, cartridges have the great disadvantage that you cannot tell by looking at them whether or not they have blown. So, you must replace each cartridge, one by one, and check each time to see if the circuit is working again.

It is well worth keeping everything you need to mend fuses in a safe place close to the fuseboxes, particularly as you will probably be fumbling about in the pitch dark. A torch that works, fuse wire (or spare cartridges), and an electrical screwdriver are enough. If you want to be extra efficient you might consider buying spare fuse holders from your local electricity board and wiring them up so that they are all ready to replace any blown fuse quickly. You could then mend the blown fuse at your leisure, after the power is back on.

Circuit breakers

Some modern electrical installations use gadgets called circuit breakers instead of fuses. These are simply switches that automatically turn themselves off if the circuit is overloaded or short circuited.

With circuit breakers there is no need to fumble with screwdrivers and little bits of fiddly wire. Having unplugged the faulty appliance or reduced the load on the circuit, you simply check the panel of switches and flick on any in the 'off' position.

Sometimes a circuit breaker takes the form of a button that gets 'blown' out to break the circuit and only needs pressing in to reconnect the circuit.

Fuses in plugs

Square-pin plugs used in ring main installations have their own little cartridge fuses. The great advantage of this device is that if the appliance is faulty, it should blow the fuse in its own plug first and not the central fuse for the entire circuit.

Occasionally, however, this may not prove true. Depending upon which area of the circuit is affected first, the main fuse may blow instead of the plug fuse. If necessary check both fuses for repairs.

If your house is wired with a ring main, always keep a good supply of spare cartridge fuses. Although they are available with many different ratings, you only really need 3 amp and 13 amp cartridges.

Use 3-amp fuses in plugs on lamps, record players, tape recorders, clocks, power tools, electric blankets and any appliance needing less than 700 watts (check its rating by the label). For everything else, use 13-amp cartridges.

To replace the fuse in most plugs, simply unscrew the back, unclip the

blown cartridge and replace it with a new one. Then screw the plug together again.

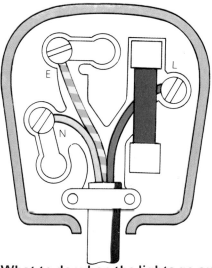

What to do when the lights go out

If you are suddenly plunged into darkness at home you will save yourself much time and energy by tracing the fault in a logical sequence. First step is to check how many lights are out.

If only one light has gone out:
1. Switch off at the wall.
2. Remove the bulb.
3. Find a bulb you know is working (if you take it from another lamp, hold it with an oven glove or cloth because it will be hot).
4. Put the new bulb in the non-functioning light and switch on.
5. If it still does not work, *switch off the mains supply* before going any further.
6. Unscrew the bulb holder to check that both wires are securely fixed. Tighten any loose screws with an electrical screwdriver.
7. If they seem O.K., unscrew the plate from the wall switch and check that the wires inside this are secure. Replace the plate.
8. Switch on at the mains.
9. If the light is still not working, call an electrician.

If more than one light has gone out:
1. Check that neighbouring houses have lights on to make sure there is not a local power failure.
2. If their lights are on, it is almost certain that a fuse has blown in your house.
3. *Switch off the mains supply* before touching the fuses.
4. Check them, one at a time, until you find which one has blown.
5. Replace the wire (see above for how to mend a fuse), push the fuse back into its socket.
6. Check the remaining fuses, in case more than one has gone.
7. Switch on the mains supply.
8. If the lights are still not working, call an electrician.

Finally, for lamps that go out, check any cartridge fuses in plugs or adaptors, in addition to the above steps.

LIGHTING

Bulbs

The great majority of bulbs used for domestic lighting in Britain have *bayonet fittings*. The two little lugs at the metal base of the bulb fit into corresponding J-shaped slots on the bulb holder. Sprung plungers in the holder keep the bulb secure and make electrical contact.

The lesser-used alternative is a *screw fitting*. You may find screw-in bulbs lighting the inside of your refrigerator, electric oven and Christmas tree lights; otherwise, they are not frequently used in the home.

Although bulbs come in all shapes and sizes, their components are basically the same; a coiled tungsten filament normally gives off the light. In a clear bulb you should be able to see whether or not the filament is complete — obviously, if it is broken at any point the bulb is useless. With opaque bulbs you can sometimes see up through a rim of clear glass around the base. Alternatively, if there is a dry rattling sound when you give the bulb a gentle shake, it is probably blown.

Most tungsten bulbs are either pear-shaped or mushroom-shaped. Mushroom bulbs are smaller and neater, but give off the same amount of heat as a pear-shaped bulb.

Never put a bulb with a wattage higher than the maximum recommended by the manufacturer, into a light fitting. Many modern light fittings can easily be damaged by the heat from too powerful a bulb. If this danger exists, the recommended wattage is always marked on the fitting.

When you are replacing a blown bulb, remember to give it time to cool, or to protect your hands with an oven glove or cloth. Even low wattage electric light bulbs get extremely hot and can easily give you a nasty burn.

The average life expectancy of a bulb is alleged by manufacturers to be between 800 and 1000 hours, although it is the sort of claim that many householders may view with some scepticism. Some bulbs do not seem to last more than about 10 minutes, and the other maddening aspect is that when they go, they all seem to go together — so in the space of a week you find you need about a dozen replacement bulbs.

If a bulb explodes or breaks off in the holder it can be tricky to remove. Before you try anything, *switch off the mains supply*. Then clear away any splinters of glass to minimize the risk of cuts. It if is impossible to get your fingers around the metal base to edge it out, use a blunt instrument with a broad blade, preferably made of wood or rubber, to probe into the centre of the bulb base. With a bayonet fitting, first press down to release the lugs from the hook of the 'J', then turn in an anti-clockwise direction until you feel the plungers pushing the base out. If it is a screw fitting bulb, just turn in an anti-clockwise direction.

Fluorescent tubes

Fluorescent tubes have either a bayonet fitting at each end or a two-pin plug.

To replace a bayonet-fitting tube, slide back the socket covers at each end to expose the lamp holder. Press the tube at each end against the spring-loaded holder, twist and remove. Twist anti-clockwise when you are removing a tube and clockwise when you are replacing one.

Two-pin tubes have plugs on hinged brackets at each end. To remove the tube, hold it with one hand and ease out one of the end brackets to disconnect the pins.

All fluorescent tubes have an automatic switch known as a 'starter', normally located on top of the lamp holder. It is a little round plug, easily removed by twisting anti-clockwise.

If the tube glows white at each end when you switch it on but does not light completely, the starter is faulty and should be replaced. If the tube flickers constantly or keeps switching on and off, it could also be the starter at fault, particularly if the tube is fairly new. (Fluorescent tubes have a working life of between 5,000 and 7,000 hours and should last from three to five years.) A swirling effect along the tube is normal in a new light, but if it persists it, too, could mean the starter needs replacing.

If a tube starts to blacken a few inches from the end, it means the electrode material inside is evaporating and, consequently, the tube will soon fail. Tubes that glow red at each end and old tubes that flicker should be replaced.

Changing a broken lamp holder

Chipped or broken lamp holders are dangerous, particularly if they are taking the weight of a heavy shade. It is not difficult to replace them.

First, switch off the mains. Take out the bulb and remove the shade by unscrewing the first (or lowest) ring. Hold the bottom of the lamp holder and unscrew the top cover to expose the terminals. Loosen the two little screws holding the wires and pull them clear.

Refit the new lamp holder in the reverse order, making sure that you pull the flex through the cover before connecting up the terminals. Strip the outer insulation from the wires before making the connections, as you would when fixing a plug (see page 13).

Take care when you are replacing

When wiring a conventional ceiling light fitting, be sure to connect the appropriate flex to the proper cable wire in the ceiling.

the cover and the shade holder that you screw them on straight — it is sometimes easy to cross the threads, in which case they will stick and you will not be able to tighten them.

Fairy Lights

Christmas tree lights are notoriously temperamental and never seem to work when you want them to (i.e. when you drag them out from wherever they have been hidden all year). Most of them are wired in such a way that if one bulb blows or disconnects, the whole string goes out. With screw fitting bulbs, the most frequent cause of failure is a bulb becoming loose — the remedy is to tighten one bulb after another until they come on again.

If a faulty bulb is the cause of the blackout, the problem is to work out which one has gone. The only way to do it is to start at the beginning, replacing one bulb after another until they go on again. You only need one spare bulb to test for the failure. If you fit it into a place and the lights do not come on, you can assume the bulb in your hand is all right and that the fault is further down the line.

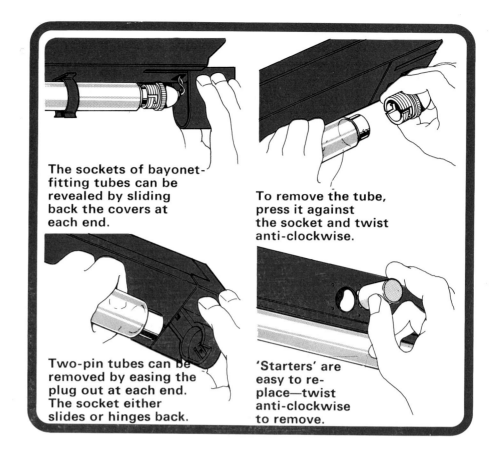

The sockets of bayonet-fitting tubes can be revealed by sliding back the covers at each end.

To remove the tube, press it against the socket and twist anti-clockwise.

Two-pin tubes can be removed by easing the plug out at each end. The socket either slides or hinges back.

'Starters' are easy to re-place—twist anti-clockwise to remove.

Below: Fluorescent tubes exposed. Bayonet-fitting tubes are less common today, but adaptors are available to convert the fitting to take the more usual two-pin tubes.

Starter

Two-pin fitting

Bayonet-fitting

IF AN APPLIANCE WILL NOT WORK

Never attempt to do any repairs on an appliance until you have disconnected all plugs from sockets. Any switches should be turned to the 'off' position.

First, what isn't working — the socket, plug or appliance?

To check the socket, plug in another appliance and see if that works. If it does not, it means there is no power at the socket. Turn off the mains switches and check the fuses. If they all seem O.K., keep the mains off and unscrew the front of the socket outlet to make sure all the wires at the back are securely connected. Replace the socket and switch on the mains. If it still does not work, call an electrician.

If the socket is working, *check the plug.* Unscrew the back and ensure that all the wires are firmly fixed to the terminals. If it is a square pin plug, take out the cartridge fuse and clip in a replacement of the same rating. Fix the plug together and try the appliance again. If it is still not working, the wire from the plug to the appliance, or the appliance itself, must be faulty.

Electric kettles

If a kettle ceases to operate, first check the connections *inside the plug at the kettle end*. A single screw in the end of the plug releases a collar which can be pushed back to expose the connections inside. If they are securely fixed, then the fault is in the wire itself, or the element inside the kettle has gone.

If the *wire* looks frayed and worn, that may be where the fault lies, and, in any case, it should be replaced. Buy a new length of 'non-kinking flex' (it is covered with a fine fabric mesh) and fit a plug for a socket at one end. Before removing the old wire, make a careful note of how the kettle plug is connected — a diagram may be useful. Bare the ends of the new flex, no more than $\frac{1}{2}$ inch (13 mm), slip the

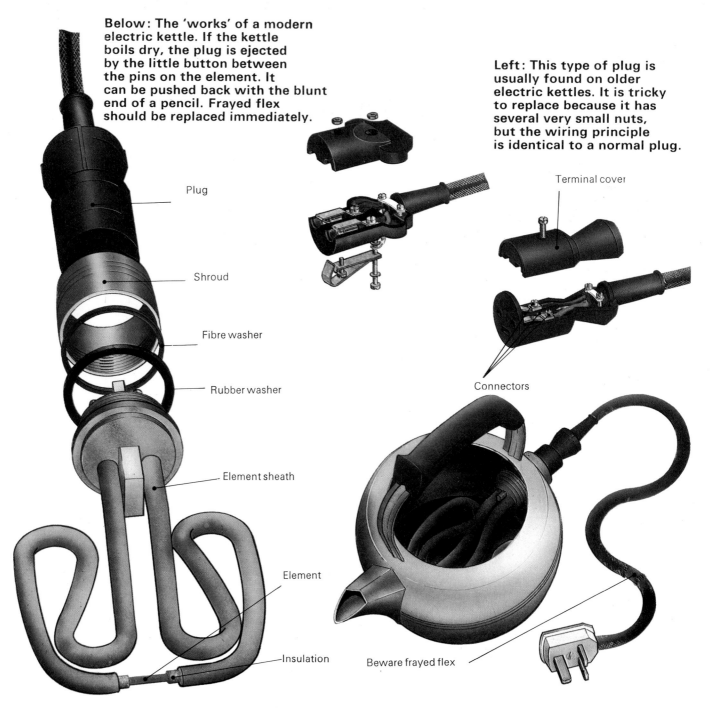

Below: The 'works' of a modern electric kettle. If the kettle boils dry, the plug is ejected by the little button between the pins on the element. It can be pushed back with the blunt end of a pencil. Frayed flex should be replaced immediately.

Plug

Shroud

Fibre washer

Rubber washer

Element sheath

Element

Insulation

Left: This type of plug is usually found on older electric kettles. It is tricky to replace because it has several very small nuts, but the wiring principle is identical to a normal plug.

Terminal cover

Connectors

Beware frayed flex

collar over the flex and *re-connect exactly as it was before*. Push the collar back over the plug and secure it with the screw.

If it is the *element* that is faulty, it is not difficult to replace. Hold the element inside the kettle with one hand and unscrew the metal 'shroud' over the socket outside the kettle. Between the shroud and the kettle there will be a *fibre washer* which you need not bother to keep — a new one is always supplied with the new element.

With the shroud unscrewed you will be able to remove the element from the kettle. Take it with you when you buy a replacement — it is important that it is the same.

The new element will have a *rubber sealing washer* which fits between the element and the inside of the kettle. Slip it over the thread then put the element in the kettle and push the end through the hole in the side. Fit a new *fibre washer outside*, then screw back the shroud tightly so that no water can leak through the joint. Make sure the *element* is *parallel* with the bottom of the kettle and not touching it, or it may burn out quickly.

Vacuum cleaners

Most vacuum cleaner repairs should be undertaken by a qualified electrician or a dealer. So if, after checking the fuse and plug connections, a vacuum still refuses to work, there is very little you can do except to call in outside help.

If the motor is working, however, but the vacuum is not cleaning particularly well, first check that the dust bag does not need emptying.

With a *cylinder-type cleaner*, a split in the hose can cause considerable loss of efficiency. You can make a temporary repair by binding it tightly with masking tape or plastic insulation tape. If the hose becomes blocked, you can probably clear it by fitting it to the blowing end of the cleaner and putting the nozzle in the suction end.

Upright cleaners have a roller brush which is driven by a rubber belt. If either become worn, the cleaner will not work properly. Most dealers stock replacements which you can fit yourself.

First, unclip the cover plate from the front of the cleaner and pull the belt off the drive shaft. Lay the cleaner on its side and undo the screws which hold the metal shield under the roller. Lift out the brush and belt (there may be a little catch at one end of the roller which frees it) and fit the replacements. Do not forget that the *drive belt* must be slipped *over* the *roller before* it is put back into place. And when you re-fasten the drive belt over the drive shaft, twist it *clockwise*. If you put it on the other way it will slip off as soon as you start the cleaner. Often items like pins or hair in the roller or belt impair the cleaner's efficiency.

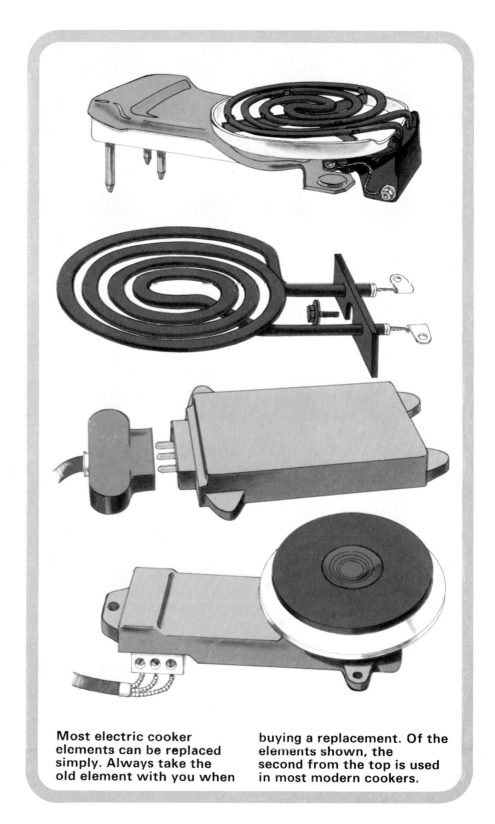

Most electric cooker elements can be replaced simply. Always take the old element with you when buying a replacement. Of the elements shown, the second from the top is used in most modern cookers.

Electric cookers

Hotplate elements on electric cookers can be replaced if they stop working. Lift the hinged top of the cooker and unscrew the plate covering the element terminals. Unplug the cooker first.

Unscrew the terminals of the faulty element and undo the nuts holding the bracket which supports the element. Lift the element out from the top and fit the new one, of *exactly* the same type in the reverse order.

For different types of elements, follow the manufacturers instructions.

Liquidizers and mixers

Some models have automatic cut-out switches which turn off the appliance if you ask too much of it — if you are trying to liquidize too thick or too heavy a substance, for example.

So if a liquidizer or mixer suddenly stops in mid-operation, first look for a cut-out switch. It is liable to be a little red button in the base of the appliance. *Do not* press it back and try to finish the job. Obviously, whatever you are trying to do is too difficult for the appliance.

Irons

The flex on an iron can quickly become frayed and worn because it is subjected to considerable twisting and friction. If it is not replaced, the wire inside the flex will eventually break or cause a short circuit.

Most irons have an insulating plate fixed in place by a single screw covering the connections. Make sure the iron is unplugged, then take off this cover. Take a careful note of the way the wires are connected before you disconnect them.

Use 'non-kinking flex' of the same length to replace the worn flex and re-connect it *exactly* as it was before. *Before* you connect up, however, slip the rubber sleeve over the flex.

If you are replacing a defective part, make certain you take it along with you when you buy a replacement.

ELECTRIC FIRES

About the only thing that can go wrong with most electric fires is the element — and it is normally simple to replace. *An element* in an electric fire is a special coil of wire which glows hot when current passes through it. It may be protected and enclosed by silica-glass tubing, or it may be completely exposed — either wrapped around an insulating rod or stretched across a rectangular piece of fireclay.

If your electric fire is not working, *first*, as usual, check the plug connections and fuses. If they are all right; then you will need to replace the element. *Always unplug the fire first.*

Enclosed elements
Unscrew or unclip the guard over the reflector. The terminals are usually covered by insulating sleeves — squeeze them on both sides to free them and slide them clear. Undo the nut at each end of the element ridges and lift it clear. Replace the new element in the reverse order.

Fireclay elements
Undo the back of the fire and loosen the terminal screws holding the wires in place. Pull the wires free. Remove the nuts holding the unit in place and remove the unit. Take it with you when you buy a replacement to make sure it is the same size and type. Replace in the reverse order.

Bowl reflectors
Unclip the fireguard and unscrew the two retaining screws beside the element in the reflector bowl. Ease off the box at the back, disconnect the terminals and remove the element. Take it with you when you buy a replacement. Refit in the reverse order.

Fan heaters and convector fires
Both these types of heaters have more complicated elements that cannot be replaced at home. If they do not work, check the plug connection and fuses. Be sure to clean and dust them regularly. If they still do not work, take them to a qualified electrician for repair.

'Flame-effect' fires
The 'burning coal' effect in some electric fires is created very simply by a low wattage bulb with a piece of polished metal suspended above it which revolves from the heat of the bulb. If it goes out, replace the bulb.

Extending flex
Very often new appliances are not supplied with sufficient flex for you

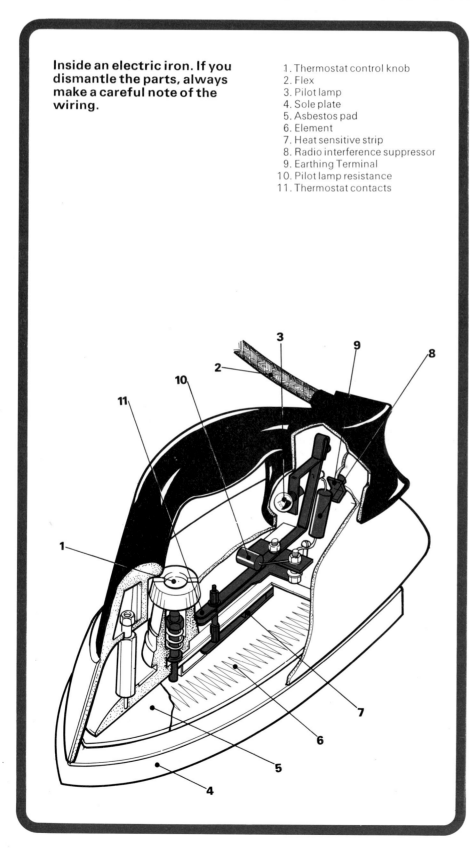

Inside an electric iron. If you dismantle the parts, always make a careful note of the wiring.

1. Thermostat control knob
2. Flex
3. Pilot lamp
4. Sole plate
5. Asbestos pad
6. Element
7. Heat sensitive strip
8. Radio interference suppressor
9. Earthing Terminal
10. Pilot lamp resistance
11. Thermostat contacts

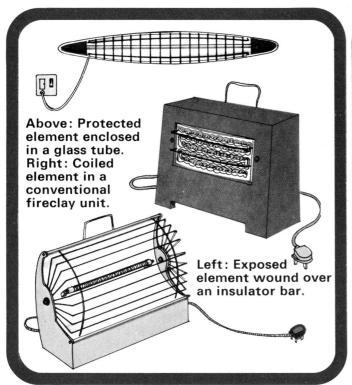

Above: Protected element enclosed in a glass tube. Right: Coiled element in a conventional fireclay unit.

Left: Exposed element wound over an insulator bar.

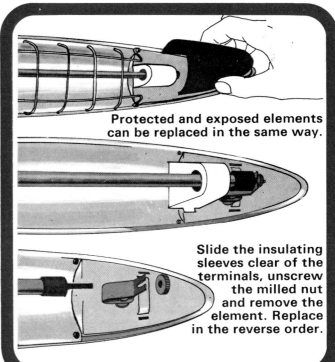

Protected and exposed elements can be replaced in the same way.

Slide the insulating sleeves clear of the terminals, unscrew the milled nut and remove the element. Replace in the reverse order.

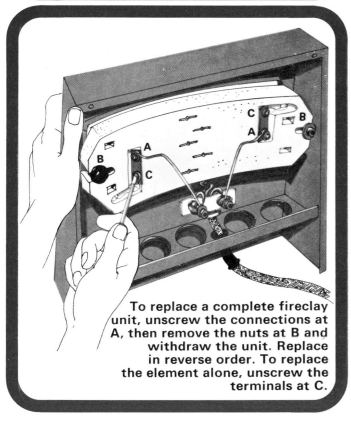

To replace a complete fireclay unit, unscrew the connections at A, then remove the nuts at B and withdraw the unit. Replace in reverse order. To replace the element alone, unscrew the terminals at C.

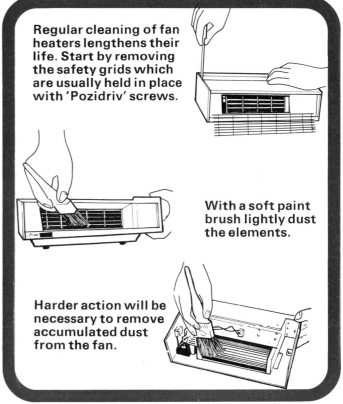

Regular cleaning of fan heaters lengthens their life. Start by removing the safety grids which are usually held in place with 'Pozidriv' screws.

With a soft paint brush lightly dust the elements.

Harder action will be necessary to remove accumulated dust from the fan.

---

to be able to position the appliance where you want it and still be able to plug it in. Never extend flex. Buy a new length which matches the colour and size of the existing flex. Remove the plug and fix it at one end of the new flex. Remove the old short length of flex from the appliance and connect the new flex in exactly the same way.

Safety
DO NOT
. . . attempt any repairs unless the appliance is unplugged or the mains supply is switched off.
. . . touch electrical equipment with wet hands or feet, or use it while standing barefoot on a wet floor.
. . . use electric heaters without guards over the bars.
. . . run flex under the carpet.
. . . allow flex to become frayed and worn.
. . . light cigarettes or paper from electric fire elements.
. . . re-wire any appliance unless you are sure you know what you are doing.
. . . overload sockets with multi-plug adaptors.
. . . use anything but the right thickness of wire to mend a fuse.
. . . connect the neutral wire to a live terminal or vice versa.
. . . fix nails into walls near switches or sockets, or through floors where cable may be positioned.
. . . take chances. ELECTRICITY CAN BE DANGEROUS.

GAS

Probably the best advice that can be given about gas appliances is to *leave them well alone*. The few simple maintenance and repair jobs that can be safely tackled at home are shown here — any other work required should be undertaken by your local gas board.

Leaks
Gas is potentially lethal and explosive. If you think you can smell gas in the home, do not waste time. First check your gas cooker to make certain that none of the burners have blown out. If the cooker has a pilot light, make sure it is still burning.

If the cooker is not guilty, check all the other gas appliances in the house, making sure the taps are turned off tightly and pilot lights are still burning.

If the smell of gas is still strong, *turn off the main gas tap (next to the meter), extinguish all naked flames*, and telephone the gas board immediately. Open windows for ventilation.

If you only *think* you can smell gas, but you are not sure, there is a simple way to check for a leak. Turn off all the

gas appliances in the house, including all pilot lights. Then, look at the gas meter. The pointer in the large top dial should be quite still. Mark its position and check it again in 20 minutes. If it's still in the same place, the smell might be in your imagination. If it has moved, however slightly, there is a leak somewhere — telephone the gas board and open some windows.

Caution. If you still smell gas and the meter does not move, call the gas board — the leak may not always register on the meter.

Never look for a gas leak with a match, lighter or any other naked flame. It may sound a bit like a scene from Laurel and Hardy, but people do still do it.

Apart from piped-in domestic gas, bottled gas can also be dangerous when used with a poorly regulated burner which causes it to burn and give off carbon monoxide.

Cookers
Replacements for broken burners and burner jets can be bought at your local gas showroom. Use a stiff bristle brush and a damp cloth to clean burner holes if necessary.

If the *automatic ignition* fails to work, the pilot light has probably blown out or the jet has become blocked. If blockage occurs, contact your local gas board. Do not use a pin pricker or needle to clear the jet — this could cause damage.

Water heaters
The front panel of modern gas water heaters can usually be moved to allow for occasional cleaning of the pilot flame jet. If you pull off the two control knobs, the casing should lift clear. Do not attempt to clean the jet with a pin or pricker.

On older heaters, pipes have to be removed before the casing will come away. *Do not* fiddle with this type, unless you are a gas fitter.

Convector heaters
Prick the jet and clean inside convector heaters once a year. The automatic ignition on many models is powered by batteries which need replacing from time to time. You may find them underneath the heater, held in place by a locating clip, or mounted in a case behind the front covering panel.

Radiant fires
The white clay bars which glow and retain the heat from the burner jets in radiant fires are called, appropriately enough, radiants. They are quite brittle and will snap if accidentally knocked or kicked. There are two types — box radiants and bar radiants.

To replace them, first unclip the fireguard (if there is one). With a *box radiant*, lift it first, then ease the bottom out of the locating slot and slide it out.

Blocked gas jets can be cleaned with a stiff bristle brush. If further work is required, a qualified gas fitter should be contacted.

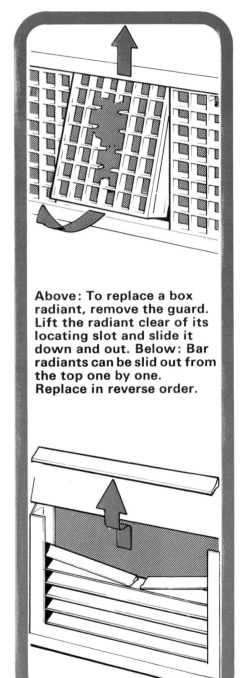

Above: To replace a box radiant, remove the guard. Lift the radiant clear of its locating slot and slide it down and out. Below: Bar radiants can be slid out from the top one by one. Replace in reverse order.

Reverse the process to replace the new radiant.

To get at a broken *bar radiant*, start at the top sliding each one up and out, one by one, until you reach the broken bar. Replace the good ones and put the new one on top.

In both cases it is worth taking the broken radiant to the gas showrooms when you buy a replacement to ensure that you get the same size and design.

'Flame effect' gas fires
If the imitation coal or logs suddenly stop 'burning', unplug the fire and lift off the 'fire effect' panel. The 'flames' are created by metal discs revolving in the heat of a low-wattage electric bulb. Lift off the disc and replace the bulb to start the 'fire' going again.

WHAT YOU CAN DO ABOUT DAMP

The very word 'damp' seems to strike terror into the heart of the average householder. It's quite unnecessary — dampness in a house can always be remedied and in many cases it can be done very simply and cheaply, provided the cause can be recognized.

You will know damp when you see it. The first indication is a group of little black spots appearing on the wallpaper or plaster. The little black spots grow into big black spots which become great damp patches. Wallpaper will start peeling off, and you are liable to notice a distinctly unpleasant smell. Something, obviously, has to be done about it.

Shown here are the causes of damp that you can do something about. If none of them apply to your particular damp problem, you will need to call in outside help. There are many specialist firms now developing cheap and fast methods of curing damp. It is always worth getting at least two estimates. But first, be sure you cannot cope with it yourself . . .

Common external sources

The most common source of damp is the ground underneath your feet. If damp is coming into the house because the damp proof course (dpc) between the ground and the house structure has failed, then there is absolutely nothing you can do about it.

But there are ways of damp 'jumping' the damp proof course. Earth heaped up against an exterior wall over the level of the dpc will enable damp to penetrate and start rising up the wall. If you move the earth away from the wall you will solve the problem.

Houses with wooden ground floors need ventilation under the floor to prevent dampness caused by condensation. This ventilation is provided by air bricks set into the wall under the level of the floor. Air bricks can either be ordinary-looking bricks with a series of round holes through them, or little perforated gratings. Because they have to be set low in the wall, they often become clogged by soil or plants. Keep them clear and you will prevent dampness under the floor.

A path close to the house, even slightly below the dpc, can cause problems if heavy rain splashes on to the path and then on to the walls

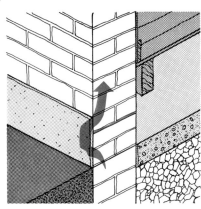

An exterior rendering applied for decorative effect can negate the damp proof course. Here it is enabling damp to rise above the dpc. The simple remedy is to chip away the rendering until it is about an inch below the dpc.

Keen gardeners intent on a little amateur landscaping can also unintentionally ruin the effectiveness of a damp-proof course. Earth piled against wall can allow damp to penetrate into the house. Remedy: remove the earth.

A cavity wall will only keep damp out when the cavity is perfect. If it is bridged by mortar or rubble left by a sloppy builder, damp can enter the house. Only a damp-proofing expert can provide a remedy to this problem.

Fortunately, this kind of building is rarely encountered now. The dpc has been laid at different levels in the brickwork, resulting in a gap. The professional remedy is to join the two levels with a vertical section.

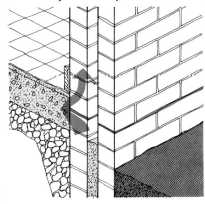

A solid floor has been laid inside a house above the level of the dpc. Since it has no insulating membrane, damp rising through the floor hits the interior walls. The only solution is to re-lay the floor on a polythene membrane.

Left: Most houses built before 1900 had no form of dpc included; ground floor rooms were often very damp as a result. Right: An incomplete dpc is as bad as none at all. The wall must be totally insulated from the ground.

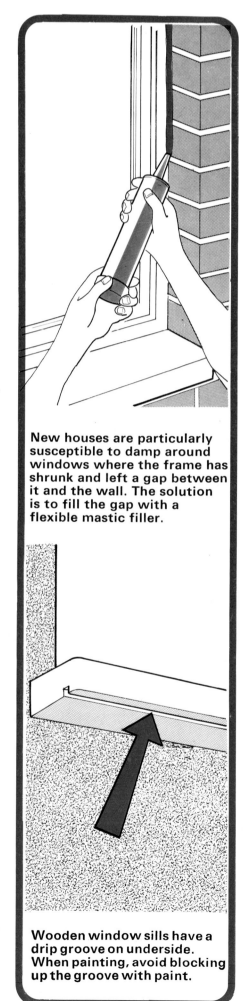

New houses are particularly susceptible to damp around windows where the frame has shrunk and left a gap between it and the wall. The solution is to fill the gap with a flexible mastic filler.

Wooden window sills have a drip groove on underside. When painting, avoid blocking up the groove with paint.

above the damp proof course. If you cannot lower the path (and that's likely to be a hefty job) you can solve the problem by painting a damp-repellant liquid onto the brickwork. It need go no higher than about a foot. Your local builders' merchant will be able to supply a suitable product — there are many on the market.

If you notice damp around window and door frames, what has probably happened (particularly in new houses) is that the frame has shrunk and left a gap between it and the wall into which damp can penetrate. The easiest way to seal this gap is to buy a tube of flexible mastic and simply squeeze it in between the frame and the wall. Do not use putty because it will harden and eventually break away, or an interior grade cellulose filler, such as Polyfilla, because it is not waterproof.

Another common cause of damp underneath windows is that the 'drip groove' has been blocked by paint. A drip groove is cut all the way along the underside of many window sills to prevent rain running under the sill and into the wall. If you scratch out the paint in the groove (or whatever is blocking it) you will solve the problem.

Condensation

If damp appears on your walls on cold, dry days when it has not rained for some time, the problem is almost certainly not damp coming in from outside, but damp being generated on the inside by condensation. Condensation occurs when warm, moisture-laden air comes into contact with cold, non-porous surfaces like windows or painted walls. It is most common in bathrooms and kitchens where steam adds to the humidity of the air.

A certain cure for condensation is to get an extractor fan fitted, but that you cannot do yourself. What you can do is to insulate the ceiling by covering it with stick-on expanded polystyrene tiles. They are very cheap and easy to fix, but be sure to buy the fire-resistant variety. The less expensive variety are highly flammable.

If you are using an oil heater in a room with condensation problems, this alone could be the cause of damp problems. Oil heaters release a huge amount of water vapour into the air — at least a gallon of water for every gallon of paraffin burned. Change the heater and you may cure the problem.

In bathrooms there is another, even simpler, remedy for reducing condensation. It requires a shower attachment of some sort. Run the cold water into the bath first, then run the hot water in under the cold, *via* the shower. It will cut down enormously on the amount of steam coming from the bath.

HOW TO STOP DRAUGHTS AND STAY WARM

If you can never seem to get your house suitably warm in cold weather, the first thing to think about is not how much heating you have, but where the heat is going.

A careful examination of houses in many countries, including Great Britain, will show that large numbers are built without sufficient insulation. This can mean that even if you have full central heating, and roaring open fires and half a dozen electric heaters in every room, you could still feel cold.

In fact, up to three quarters of your fuel bills could be going towards heating the air *outside*. It has been calculated that in an average semi detached house with central heating but no proper insulation, 25 per cent of the heat goes through the outside walls, 20 per cent through the roof, 20 per cent through the windows, doors and chimneys and 10 per cent through the ground floor.

There is much that you can do to improve the insulation of your home, and whatever you may spend on draught proofing or do-it-yourself insulation, you will most probably save in a year or two on fuel bills.

Roof

All heat rises, so without a properly insulated roof you will never be able to get your house warm; the heat will simply float up straight through the upstairs' ceilings into the attic and out through the roof tiles. Nice for the birds, but not for you.

Insulating a roof sounds like a major job, but it's not. Neither is it difficult or expensive — it's just likely to be awkward and a bit dirty. Most houses have access to the attic space through a 'hatch' in an upstairs' ceiling — usually above the landing. If you can get up there, you can do the job.

Heat escapes through the thin plasterboard which is nailed to joists and forms the upstairs ceiling (see page 7). It is the space between the joists that has to be insulated.

The most popular, and simplest, methods of insulating are either to lay rolls of thick mineral wool or glass fibre between the joists, or to fill the gaps with loose granules of insulating material, such as Vermiculite.

Usually, you can buy rolls of glass fibre in the right width to fill the gap completely, but it is unpleasant to handle and you should wear gloves. The 'loose-fill' insulation you can buy in sacks. It looks like a particularly unpleasant breakfast cereal, but it is very light and, consequently, not difficult to handle. The only possible difficulty is in making sure that you get an even layer, at least two inches (50 mm) thick. You can do this by cutting a piece of cardboard to act as a 'rake' for the material.

Hints and precautions
Remember while you are up in the attic, only step on the thick wooden joists, never on the plasterboard underneath them. Plasterboard has very little inherent strength and cannot support the weight of an adult.

Another important precaution is never to insulate the area underneath the cold water cistern, otherwise the water in the cistern will freeze solid at the first sign of really cold weather (normally, the heat you are losing from the house prevents it from freezing up).

While you are up in the attic, it is worth doing a proper job by insulating the cistern itself and 'lagging' the pipes. If you are using rolls of insulation, just wrap the tank and pipes around snugly and tie them up with string like a parcel. Leave a small air hole at the top.

Your hot water tank should also be wrapped up in the same way, but you will probably find it easier to buy a tailored 'jacket' of thick padding which simply straps or ties around the tank. In a week this insulation will conserve enough heat for at least 10 baths.

All the materials you will need for this work are readily available at

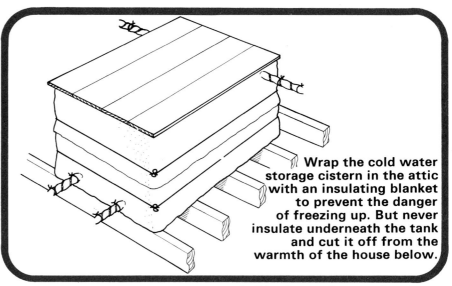

Wrap the cold water storage cistern in the attic with an insulating blanket to prevent the danger of freezing up. But never insulate underneath the tank and cut it off from the warmth of the house below.

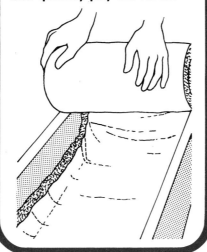

Rolls of fibreglass laid between the joists in the attic will cut down enormously on the amount of heat lost through the roof and quickly pay for itself.

builders' merchants. Certain consumers' associations have figured that you may save the cost of roof insulating material within two years.

Floors and walls
Unfortunately, there is not a great deal you can do to prevent heat loss through floors and walls. Underlays and carpets on the ground floor will certainly help stop heat escaping downwards, but if you have draughts whistling up through the floorboards, the only simple way of stopping them is by filling the gaps with plastic wood. This is a boring, laborious job and the visual effect may not be too pleasing. Whether it is worth while, only you can tell — it depends how bad the draughts are and how much you value your comfort.

Lining walls with sheets of expanded polystyrene before wallpapering improves insulation to some extent, but has disadvantages. First it adds to the cost, time and trouble you must take to re-decorate a room, and secondly, it crushes easily and if you

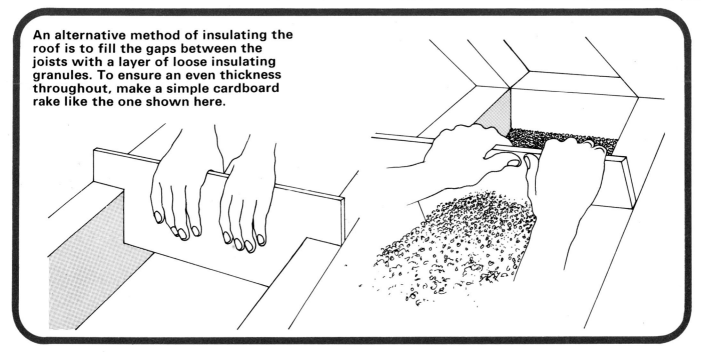

An alternative method of insulating the roof is to fill the gaps between the joists with a layer of loose insulating granules. To ensure an even thickness throughout, make a simple cardboard rake like the one shown here.

bump against it, the surface of the wall will begin to look uneven. Be sure to buy the fire-resistant variety.

Draughts

Draughts, unfortunately, are not only found in old houses. Even newly built houses develop cracks and gaps — due either to shrinkage or poor workmanship—through which the cold wind can howl. Fortunately for you, however, it is generally possible to make big improvements where draughts are concerned, at little cost or effort.

You will be able to tell roughly where draughts are coming from. To find the exact spot, strike a match and hold it around the frames of doors and windows. When the flame leans horizontally away from the frame, or blows out, you have found the problem.

Doors

The main source of draughts in most homes is from gaps under doors. The simplest, but just about the most inconvenient, remedy is to stitch a long fabric sausage and stuff it against the gap when the door is closed. However,

the irritation suffered all around by the constant need to replace the sausage every time the door is opened and closed makes it hardly worth the effort.

A much better idea is to have a draught excluder actually attached to the door. There are dozens of different proprietary designs on the market, but again none of them is very beautiful or unobtrusive. The cheapest and simplest variety is a stick-on plastic strip with a flap of felt covering the gap between door and floor. One disadvantage here is that the flap is liable to drag on the carpet and may become so loose that draughts can still push their way under it.

A better solution is a strip with a flap which rises up to clear the carpet when the door is opened. There are several types which do this, and they are easy to fit, providing you can nail reasonably straight.

To seal gaps around the sides and tops of doors, you may use a stick-on, foam plastic strip for a quick, cheap remedy. These are very easy to fit, but do tend to come unstuck after a while, so will need replacing more frequently than other draughtproofing methods. They are also apt to become extremely dirty and are difficult to clean.

Much more durable is a V-shaped metal strip which is very springy, and, as the door closes, jams tight between the door and frame. Those that have to be nailed around the frame are, in fact, quite tricky to fit — but there are versions of the same idea that can be glued on. With careful fixing, this type of draught excluder looks neat and unobtrusive and will last for years.

If you have very wide, uneven gaps all around the door, the best way to stop them up is to use rubber or plastic 'buffer' tubing. This may look cumbersome, especially if you have to fix it on the outside of the frame, but at least it works.

flaps can be purchased to screw over the back of the letter box, but a thick piece of leather or felt tacked on to the top edge will work just as well (see below).

Windows

Draughts from ordinary wooden frame windows can be stopped with the same stick-on, foam plastic strip or V-shaped metal strip used for doors. Metal windows are a bit more of a problem, but there is now generally available a system of pre-formed aluminium strips which can be cut with scissors then snapped on over the frame.

Lined and interlined curtains will do a great deal to keep the cold at bay when they are drawn across windows. And, they will work even better if they are lined with *Milium,* a material with a backing coat of aluminium which reflects escaping heat back into the room.

A draught excluder which lifts when the door opens can be adjusted by means of its retaining screws.

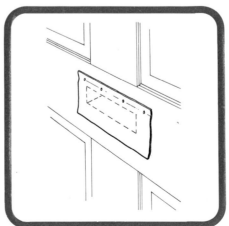

The final source of draught to check on the door is the letterbox. If the flap is loose and swings gaily in the breeze, it can easily empty all the heat out of your entrance hall and replace it with cold air. Sprung metal

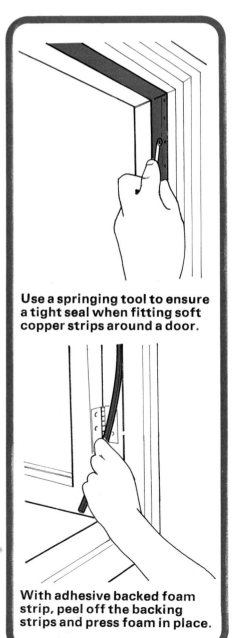

Use a springing tool to ensure a tight seal when fitting soft copper strips around a door.

With adhesive backed foam strip, peel off the backing strips and press foam in place.

PLUMBING: OVERFLOWS AND BLOCKAGES

If water starts pouring out of a pipe through the roof or an exterior wall of your house, you have an overflow. The water is coming either from *the cold water storage tank* on the roof or from a *toilet cistern* (if you have central heating, if might also be from the small expansion tank located on the roof) ; and the overflow is caused by a malfunction in the ball valve which should shut off the water supply.

First, check where the overflow is coming from by tracing the pipe to its source. If the water is pouring out on to the roof, it is almost certain to be the cold water storage tank at fault.

Repairing an overflow

To stop the overflow you must first turn off the supply of water to the tank or toilet cistern. Trace the supply pipe back until you find a tap, then turn it off (see page 6 for further details). When the water level drops below the overflow pipe outlet, it will at least stop the water from splashing outside.

A *ball valve* is composed of a hollow sphere at the end of a lever which floats on the water in the cistern. When water is drawn out of the cistern, the sphere drops and opens a valve at the end of the lever to let more water in. As the level of the water rises, so does the sphere until it eventually shuts off the valve.

Only two things can really go wrong : either the *ball float* can develop a leak, or the *washer in the valve* can wear out and fail to shut off the supply.

You can make a temporary repair to the float by shaking the water out of it and wrapping it in a plastic or polythene bag, tied tightly around the lever. The float is simply screwed on to the end of the lever, so it is easy to replace when you buy a new one.

If the washer is faulty, first take out the split pin holding the lever arm. Unscrew the cap on the end of the valve case (if there is one) and push out the piston with a screwdriver. Unscrew the two parts by holding one half with a pair of pliers and turning the other half with a screwdriver held in the slot. Lever out the small rubber washer in the small end of the piston

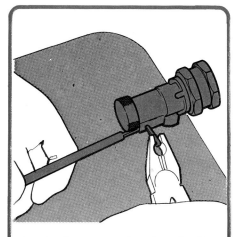

Replacing a washer in a ball valve—first take out the split pin holding the lever arm.

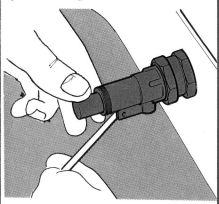

Unscrew the cap on the valve case, push out the piston with the blade of a screwdriver.

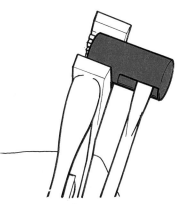

Unscrew the two parts using a pair of pliers and a screwdriver.

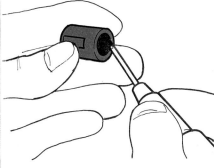

Prise the washer from the piston body and replace it with a new one.

and replace it with a new one, then screw the two parts together again. Replace the piston — washer end first — and fix the lever arm back with the split pin.

Some modern cisterns have a rubber 'diaphragm' operating against a nylon nozzle, instead of the conventional piston. To replace one of these, simply unscrew the cap at the valve end of the lever, prise loose the worn diaphragm, replace it with a new one and screw the cap back into place.

If you are worried about whether the ball float or washer is at fault, hold the lever up by hand before you turn off the water supply. If, when

Modern ball valves have rubber diaphragms, not pistons.

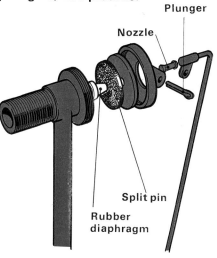

Plunger

Nozzle

Split pin

Rubber diaphragm

you hold it up, the water supply into the cistern stops, the valve is working and it is the float that is causing the trouble.

If you cannot find the tap to turn the supply off, and the workings of a ball valve are complete nonsense to you, tie the lever up with string around a piece of wood resting across the top of the cistern and call a plumber.

Blockages

All baths, basins and sinks have a grid over the waste outlet to trap solids which could block the pipe below. Nevertheless, small solids — tea leaves, hair and vegetables — can sometimes pass through the grid and cause a blockage.

To avoid this trouble, do not empty tea leaves, breadcrumbs, or anything that sets hard when wet, into your sink. If you pour hot fat down the sink, always run hot water into it for at least a minute to stop it from solidifying.

If you are stuck with a blockage, you will need a *rubber plunger* to clear it. First of all block the overflow hole at the top of the bath, basin or whatever with a wet rag to prevent air in the pipe escaping. Then see that the water in the bath, basin or sink covers

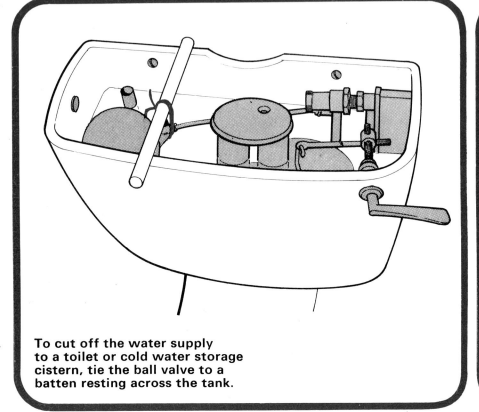

To cut off the water supply to a toilet or cold water storage cistern, tie the ball valve to a batten resting across the tank.

Plungers for clearing blockages are fitted with a metal disc to prevent the rubber cup from turning itself inside out.

the plunger cup so it will work.

Jam the plunger over the waste outlet and work the handle vigorously up and down. The alternate suction and water pressure caused by the movement of the plunger should clear the blockage. If it does, remove the rag from the overflow hole and run cold water for a minute or two to wash the blockage completely away and fill the trap.

If you do not have a plunger, you can make a reasonable substitute by wrapping a piece of cloth around a rubber sponge and tying it to the end of a pole (see diagram right).

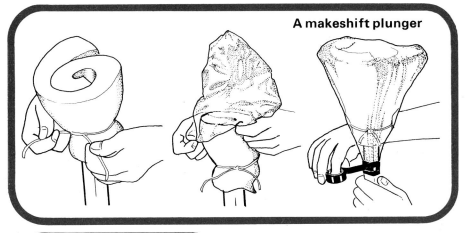

A makeshift plunger

Traps

If you still have a blockage after toiling for a few minutes with a plunger, you will have to empty the 'trap' below the sink or basin.

Most traps are U-shaped bends in the pipe, fitted with a screw plug at their lowest point. Modern plumbing installations may have 'bottle traps' which look like big plastic jars with screw caps on the bottoms.

Before you undo either, put a bucket underneath to catch the waste water. With a conventional U-trap, you should insert a bar between the U to counteract the pressure on the pipework as you unscrew the cap.

After emptying the trap, poke both sides of the pipe with a curtain wire to clear away the blockage. Replace the screw cap or plug and run cold water from the tap above to clear the pipes and re-fill the trap.

If the water is still not draining away properly, poke your curtain wire

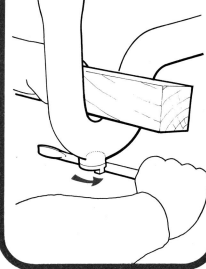

Use a simple bar to avoid undue strain on the pipes when removing a trap plug.

up the waste pipe outside the house and if that does not solve the problem, call in a plumber.

Toilet

When a toilet pan becomes blocked, you will need a special type of plunger with a metal disc fixed above it to ensure that the rubber cap is not turned inside out, inside the pan.

Insert the plunger as far down into the pan as it will go and work it up and down very quickly. As there is no flat surface to create efficient suction, it may take longer than clearing a blockage in a sink or basin. If the plunger does not work, call a plumber.

Lack of water

If by some chance your water supply should suddenly stop, check to see that someone has not accidentally turned off the stop tap located outside, or an interior stopcock. If this is not the case, call the water board.

PLUMBING: DRIPPING TAPS AND BANGING PIPES

When air spurts out of a tap along with the water or when the pipes make a terrible banging noise when you try to draw water, it indicates that there is an air lock somewhere in the system.

To cure an air lock, fix a short hose to the kitchen taps. Ensure both ends are securely fixed. Turn on the hot water first, then the cold.

Curing an air lock
One possible way to clear an air lock is to use the pressure of the mains water supply from the cold tap in the kitchen to push the water and air up through the system into the hot water cylinder.

All you need to do is to get a short length of hose. Attach one end to the cold water tap in the kitchen and the other to the hot water tap. (You may need 'jubilee clips' (bands of metal tightened by a screw) to fit the hose securely on to the taps.)

Turn on the hot water tap first,

then open the cold water tap. Let the water run for *a few seconds*, turn off the cold water tap, then the hot water tap and remove the hose.

If this does not cure the problem, it is possible to drain the whole system. However, it is wise to take professional advice before doing this to avoid creating still more air locks. Turn off the main stopcock on the rising main (see page 6) and open all the taps in the house until the water ceases to flow.

Close all the taps about two thirds, then turn on the supply. Adjust the taps to get a small, even flow of water. Then, starting at the bottom of the house, gradually open the taps more and more in rotation until all the air has spurted free.

Turn off all the taps slowly, in the same rotation, until only a dribble of water flows. Then turn them off completely.

Dripping taps
Few things are more irritating than the constant bleep bleep bleep of a dripping tap. The usual reason for a dripping tap is a worn washer, which needs replacing. Although there are a number of different kinds of taps, the process of changing a washer is more or less the same. The major variations you are likely to find are shown here.

In most houses you will probably find either *'bib taps'* or *'pillar taps'* in the kitchen and bathroom. It is easy to tell which is which — bib taps are fixed to the wall behind the sink or basin, pillar taps are fitted directly on to the sink or basin. Both work in exactly the same way, the only difference being that pillar taps have a cover which must be unscrewed before you can get at the inside.

Some modern taps — the best known are called *Supataps*—can be fitted with new washers without first turning off the water supply. Most Supataps have a handle and nozzle incorporated into one piece which points downwards into the sink.

If you are not sure which kind of tap you have, play safe by turning off the water supply first, before you attempt to change the washer.

You will probably find a stopcock underneath the sink or basin. If not, try to trace the pipe back until you come across one. If all else fails, and the hot water tap is dripping, turn off the main stopcock and drain the hot water system by opening all the taps To avoid draining the cold water cistern, turn off the stopcock which supplies the hot water cylinder.

What to do:

1. After you have turned off the supply, (and any hot water heaters, central heating boilers or such like that might burn out without water) open the tap until all the water has run out. If it does not stop, you have

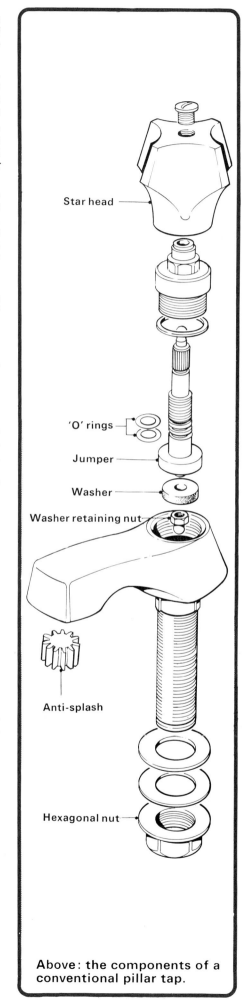

Above: the components of a conventional pillar tap.

not turned off the right stopcock. *Do not* attempt to dismantle the tap unless you can cut off the supply.

2. Unscrew the tap's cover or shield (if there is one). You may be able to do it by hand — if not, you will need an adjustable spanner or wrench. Protect the chromium plating with a rag wrapped around the jaws of the tool. Some older taps have a *reverse thread cover* — if it will not budge anti-clockwise, try turning it the other way.

3. Lift the cover clear and then undo the next nut you can see. This is the *'gland nut'* which holds the *headgear* to the *body* of the tap. Hold the tap nozzle with one hand as you turn the nut to prevent the tap from twisting. If there is not enough room between the bottom of the cover and the tap to fit in a spanner, undo the screw holding the handle, tap the handle off and remove the cover completely.

4. Lift out the headgear. The *worn washer* will either be left in the tap body or it will be held by a little nut at the very bottom of the headgear. If it is in the tap body, lift it out and replace it with a new one. If it is held in the headgear, hold the lower part steady with pliers, undo the nut, slip on a new washer and replace the nut.

5. Even if the old washers are made of leather or fibre, *always* use synthetic rubber or *nylon replacements* of the same size. If you can only get natural rubber replacements, use the *hard type* for *hot taps* and the *soft type* for *cold taps*. Always replace the washer with the side bearing the maker's name face upwards.

6. Reassemble the tap. Greasing the threads with a little lubricant jelly, such as Vaseline, will make it easier to put together and take apart next time.

Supataps

The procedure for changing a washer on Supataps is different. First, loosen the locking nut above the nozzle (hold the nozzle in one hand and turn the nut with a spanner in the other hand). Hold the nut and unscrew the complete nozzle *anti-clockwise.* Some water may come out while you are doing this, but it will stop as soon as you remove the nozzle.

Insert a screwdriver or pencil into the nozzle outlet and push out the anti-splash unit. The combined washer and 'jumper plate' is in the top of this unit. Pull it out and replace with identical parts, then reassemble the tap.

Pull-off handles

Some modern taps have large handles which must be removed before you can get access to the 'gland nut'. To

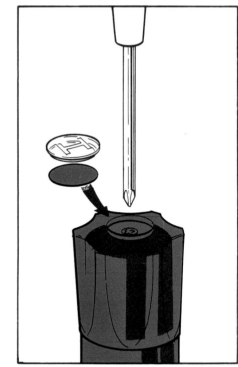

Above: To replace a washer in a tap, first remove the handle to get access to the 'gland nut'.

get the handle off, prise up the little button in the centre with a small screwdriver. Undo the screw underneath and pull off the handle. Then follow the normal procedure for changing a washer.

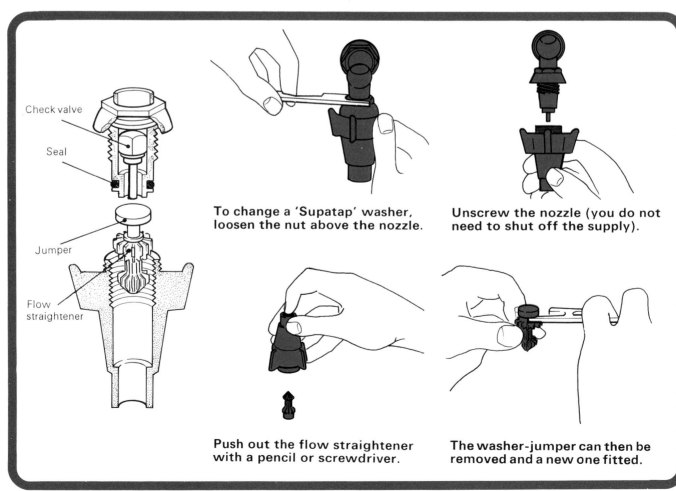

Check valve

Seal

Jumper

Flow straightener

To change a 'Supatap' washer, loosen the nut above the nozzle.

Unscrew the nozzle (you do not need to shut off the supply).

Push out the flow straightener with a pencil or screwdriver.

The washer-jumper can then be removed and a new one fitted.

PLUMBING: DRIBBLES LEAKS AND BURSTS

When water dribbles out of the top of a tap, the *gland nut* is loose. This is the nut that holds the headgear on to the body of the tap.

1. Open the tap, but do not turn off the water supply. Remove the cover to expose the gland nut. (If it is difficult, see **Dripping taps** on the previous page.)
2. Tighten the gland nut by just half a turn, using an adjustable spanner.
3. Close and open the tap to check that it moves easily. If it is too stiff, loosen the gland nut slightly.
4. Reassemble. If the tap still dribbles, turn off the supply, remove the cover and the gland nut and pack thin string rubbed in Vaseline around the spindle (the bit that holds the handle). Replace the gland nut and cover before turning on the supply.

Mixer taps
If a mixer tap dribbles from the bottom of the swivel nozzle, turn off both taps tightly but do not bother to shut off the supply. Unscrew the ring at the bottom of the nozzle — a wire clip holds the nozzle in place. Prise out the clip with a screwdriver and lift the nozzle clear. Take out the washer(s) in the base and replace. Wet the base of the nozzle before you re-fit it.

Shower fittings
When a shower fitting will not stop dripping a little rubber washer called an *O ring* needs replacing. First, turn off the water supply and open the taps until no water comes out; then unscrew the flexible shower pipe. The lever which diverts the water from the taps to the shower is held by a screw — undo it and pull off the lever. Underneath is a threaded 'connector' with a slot in the top. Push a screwdriver blade against the slot to unscrew the connector (anti-clockwise). When this is off, slide out the spindle mechanism. The 'O ring' is a black rubber ring half way along the mechanism — pull it off and replace with a new ring the same size. Reassemble in the reverse order and turn on the supply.

Leaking traps
If a trap leaks underneath a sink or basin, first check that the plug or screw cap at the bottom of the trap

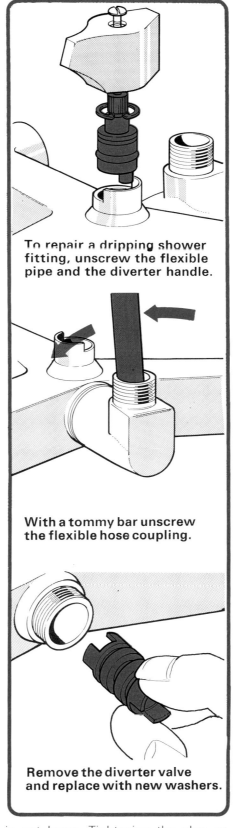

To repair a dripping shower fitting, unscrew the flexible pipe and the diverter handle.

With a tommy bar unscrew the flexible hose coupling.

Remove the diverter valve and replace with new washers.

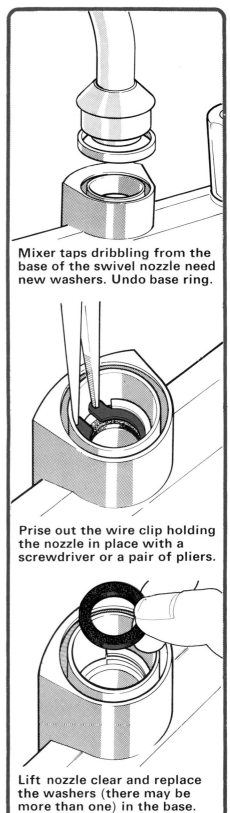

Mixer taps dribbling from the base of the swivel nozzle need new washers. Undo base ring.

Prise out the wire clip holding the nozzle in place with a screwdriver or a pair of pliers.

Lift nozzle clear and replace the washers (there may be more than one) in the base.

is not loose. Tightening the plug or cap may solve the problem, but if it does not you should fit new washers. On all traps there is a washer at the point where the trap is connected to the sink and another behind the plug or cap at the bottom of the trap. You should be able to see where the water is leaking. If not, replace both washers. With modern plastic 'bottle traps' you will be able to unscrew the connections by hand, otherwise you will need a

spanner. Make sure the replacement washers are the same size.

Leaking sink outlets
If a sink or basin leaks at the outlet, the putty sealing at the joint will have to be renewed. To remove the grating in the sink, stick a pair of pliers or strong fork into the grating to hold it steady, and unscrew the nut underneath the sink with an adjustable spanner. When the pipe is discon-

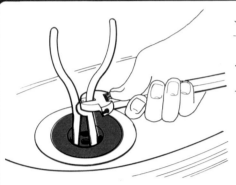

Leaking waste outlet. Undo the pipe under the sink, hold the grating steady with pliers . . .

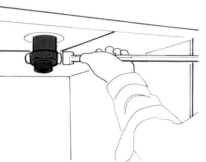

. . . and unscrew the nut under the sink with an adjustable spanner.

Lift the waste outlet clear of the sink, brush it clean and dry it.

Remove old sealing compound with a knife and clean metal surfaces with fine wire wool.

Make a new seal using fresh putty and replace the waste outlet.

Modern plastic waste outlets should be sealed with a purpose-made rubber gasket.

nected, lift the waste outlet from the sink, brush it clean and dry it thoroughly. Press putty underneath the lip all around and replace the outlet in the sink. There will be a washer underneath, where the pipe is connected. If it is worn or perished, get a replacement.

Smear putty on the washer before reconnecting the outlet pipe (you will have to hold the grating again in order to tighten the nut).

Gaps behind baths or basins

To seal a gap behind a bath or basin you will need a special flexible compound because the bath or basin tends to move slightly in use. If you try to fill the gap with putty or plaster it will soon crack and look terrible. There are a number of proprietary sealers on the market which remain elastic and, therefore, seal the gap permanently. Most of them are available in tubes and you simply squeeze the sealer into the gap. Make sure before you start, however, that you have cleaned any dirt or grease from the gap and that it is perfectly dry. After applying the sealer, trim it if necessary with a razor blade and leave it for 24 hours to set.

Nails through pipes

If you accidentally bang a nail through a pipe you will get, apart from a shock, a jet of water all over you and

the room. Obviously, the first thing you have to do is to stop it.

Do not bother putting your thumb over the burst, unless you can shout for help — it's not a particularly effective way of stopping up the leak and while you are standing there you cannot be doing what you ought to be doing.

First, if you are in the kitchen or bathroom, turn on all the taps to reduce the pressure, then *turn off the mains supply*. If you are lucky, you may be able to find a stopcock which

will isolate the particular pipe you have pierced. If you are not, you must empty the system as soon as possible.

Put a bucket underneath the burst to catch at least some of the water, then go around and turn on all the taps in the house, and flush the toilet as you pass. Be sure the mains supply is off. Turn off any water heating and plug the leak with some rags or towels until the system is drained.

Only when the water stops should you start worrying about finding a plumber.

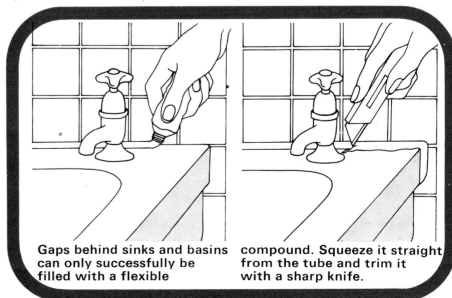

Gaps behind sinks and basins can only successfully be filled with a flexible **compound. Squeeze it straight from the tube and trim it with a sharp knife.**

PLUMBING: FREEZE UPS

How to avoid it

The best advice you can have about a freeze-up is to avoid it.

The most common cause of frozen pipes is that the house has been badly designed as far as the plumbing is concerned, and too many pipes are exposed to the elements. But short of tearing out all the pipework and starting again, there is little you can do about it.

What you can do is take a number of sensible precautions to minimize the risk. First, deal with the area of greatest risk . . . .

In the roof space all the pipes should be lagged (wrapped in insulating material) and the cold water storage tank insulated. But roof insulation should never run *under* the water tank so that it is isolated from the warmth of the house below. Draughts should be sealed off as much as possible — if necessary by lining the roof rafters with felt.

If the rising main is attached to an outside wall, that too should be lagged, particularly if it passes near an air brick.

Do not wait for cold weather before dealing with dripping taps or minor leaks; they will be the first to freeze.

Obviously, if you live in a detached house on top of a hill you run a greater risk of having a freeze-up than if you live in a flat in town. You must weigh the extent of the risk yourself, but generally, it is not a good idea to leave a house without heating of any kind for more than a few days in the depths of winter.

You do not have to keep it *warm*, but a single heater which does nothing more than take the chill out of the air could prevent you from returning to find the entire plumbing system locked by ice.

A time switch which operates an electric heater placed centrally for a few hours a night is a reasonably economic way of preventing a major freeze-up. If you know where the plumbing runs, isolate the heating to that area by shutting the doors of rooms without any plumbing in them.

However, if you plan to go away for more than a few days, it is advisable to drain the plumbing system by shutting off the stopcock on the rising main, opening all the taps and leaving them open. Dissolve a handful of salt in a pint of water and pour the mixture into the lavatory pan to stop that from freezing.

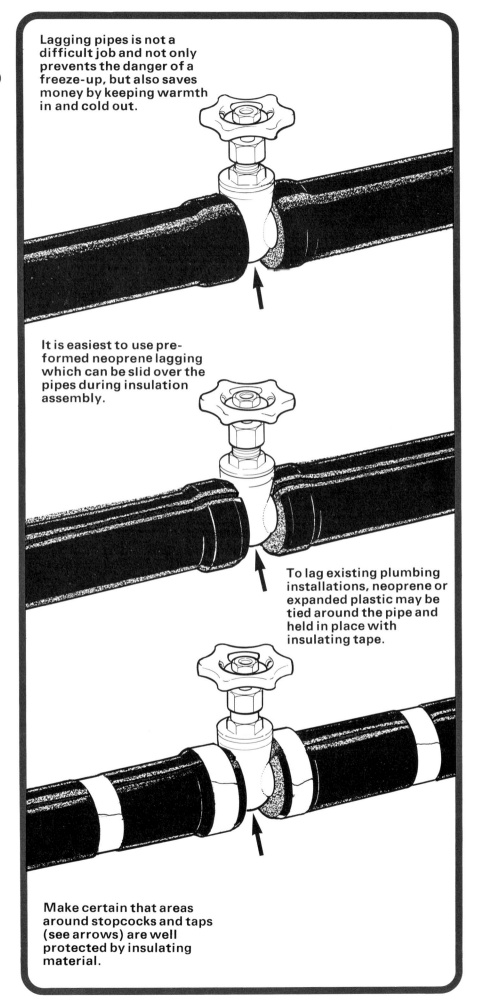

Lagging pipes is not a difficult job and not only prevents the danger of a freeze-up, but also saves money by keeping warmth in and cold out.

It is easiest to use pre-formed neoprene lagging which can be slid over the pipes during insulation assembly.

To lag existing plumbing installations, neoprene or expanded plastic may be tied around the pipe and held in place with insulating tape.

Make certain that areas around stopcocks and taps (see arrows) are well protected by insulating material.

What to do if pipes freeze up

When water freezes, its volume increases by nearly 10 per cent and so the greatest danger of a freeze-up is that the ice will swell and split the pipe. Naturally, you will not become aware of this until it has thawed.

If you wake up one morning and find that nothing happens when you turn on the tap, first try and check to see if the pipe has burst. Sometimes you can feel the split easier than you can see it; occasionally, you can see the ice glistening inside the pipe.

If all seems to be well, the problem of thawing the ice has to be tackled *gently* (too rapid a change in temperature will almost certainly split the pipe).

First, try and raise the temperature of the house by turning up the central heating or switching on additional heaters.

Then, work your way along the pipe, from the frozen tap, with hot water bottles, hot cloths or a hair drier until the ice thaws and the water runs freely again.

If none of the taps works, you will most likely find that the freeze up is in the attic — in which case you will have to grope around up there using the same process. Apply *warmth first* to the pipes supplying the system from the *cold water storage tank* (i.e. the pipes leading from the bottom of the tank.)

Burst pipes

If you are lucky (?) enough to detect a burst pipe before the ice has thawed, you can make a temporary repair by rubbing soap hard into the crack and binding the pipe tightly with adhesive tape or bandage.

Normally, however, a burst makes itself evident by spraying water out into a room in a fashion that is difficult not to notice. If the pipe is exposed (and it probably will be as it has frozen), wrap a rag tightly around the leak and put a bucket underneath to catch the spray. Then, turn the water off at the *mains* and drain the system as quickly as possible by opening all the taps. Turn off the water heating as soon as you have been around the taps.

You may only become aware of a burst when a damp patch appears on the ceiling and slightly dirty water begins to drip through an upstairs

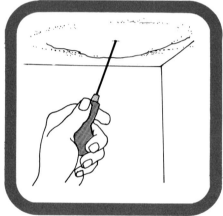

bedroom. This indicates a burst pipe in the attic. Again, turn off the mains water and start draining the system. In this instance, however, there is an additional danger — the weight of the leaking water splashing around in the attic could bring the whole ceiling down.

If you are unable to get into the attic, or if there is too much to mop up, it is usually safer to make a *small* hole in the ceiling to drain the water away (have plenty of buckets ready) than to risk the collapse of the ceiling. Small holes in plaster can be repaired (see page 44).

Cautionary note

The Water Board advise turning off your water supply at the stopcock on the rising main if you leave your house for more than a few days. It is a sensible precaution in unpredictable climates because a pipe could freeze and split, and then suddenly thaw out again. In such a case, with the water supply left on, water would pour out into your house until your return.

DRAINS AND GUTTERS

Drains inspire a particular horror among ordinary mortals, presumably because of all the nastiness that cascades down them day by day. For this same reason, they must work rather well.

Like most other elements of a house, drains are basically very simple. All rainwater from the gutters around the roof and all the waste water from baths, sinks and basins discharges first of all into a gulley set at ground level just outside the house. From there it goes, *via* a trap, to the first manhole.

Lavatory pans are connected to this same manhole, but directly, through a *soil stack* which is normally fixed to an exterior wall (although it can be inside). This stack runs underground to the manhole.

To prevent blockages, and to avoid the unpleasant task of cleaning them, be sensible about what you tip away down the sink. Tea leaves, vegetable scraps, fat, breadcrumbs and the like can all accumulate in a corner or bend and eventually block a drain.

A certain amount of kitchen waste must inevitably disappear down the sink. To minimize its effect, always flush the sink with plenty of water after washing up or preparing food. As an extra precaution, pour a bucketful of really hot water mixed with a handful of bicarbonate of soda down the kitchen waste pipe every now and again.

As a general rule, never tip anything down the drain unless it will *dissolve in cold water*, least of all things such as cellulose fillers or any kind of non-soluble powder.

The grating over the gully

The first potential blockage in the drainage system is liable to occur at the grating over the trapped gully. It is at ground level and completely open, so can easily become blocked by leaves, earth or gravel.

If this happens, lift the grating clear, scrape off the debris and scrub it before putting it back. Do not *scrape the debris into the gulley* — you may block the trap below.

Another means of cleaning the grating is to wait until you have a good garden bonfire going: put the grating into a red part of the fire for a few minutes and all the dirt will burn away.

If the grating is clear but the water is still not running away, the trap

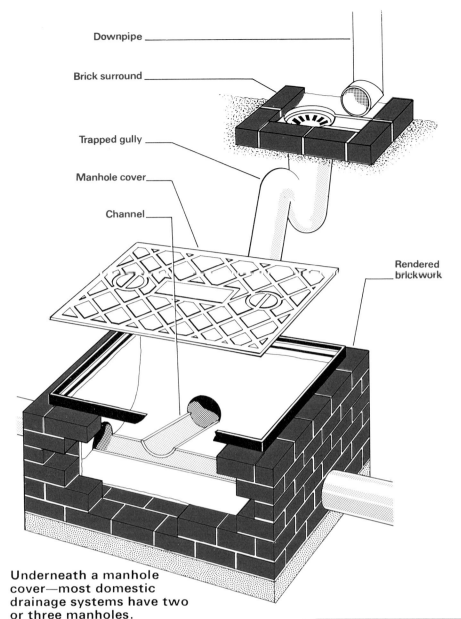

Downpipe

Brick surround

Trapped gully

Manhole cover

Channel

Rendered brickwork

Underneath a manhole cover—most domestic drainage systems have two or three manholes.

below is probably blocked. One easy way to clear it is to poke around with an old spoon tied securely to a stick. When the blocked water has drained away, empty the trap by pumping with a mop and soaking up the residue with a cloth.

Dig out any more waste solid that you can see, then rinse the gully with a few bucketfuls of very hot water mixed with washing soda. Then, run the cold water taps inside the house to make sure that the drain is quite clear before you replace the grating.

Manholes

The gully leads to the first of two, or probably three, manholes which get lower or deeper the nearer they get to the sewer. The first manhole will normally have two pipes discharging waste into it (one directly from the w.c. and the other from the basins and gutters) via the gully. It should also have an outlet pipe to carry the waste water to the next manhole, and from there to the sewer.

All manholes are covered by a metal plate with two small lifting grips at each side. It is important to keep these covers clear of weeds and debris so that they can be lifted when needed.

If clearing the grating and gully does not rid your drains of blockages, the next step in the investigation is to open the first manhole cover. It is heavy — lift it from one side only and tip it backwards. If it refuses to budge, scratch around the edges with a screwdriver and try again.

Get help if the manhole cover is too obstinate to move yourself, but once it is open you will be able to tell exactly where the blockage is: if the *chamber is empty,* the blockage

Left: Minor blockages in gullies can often be cleared by poking around with an old spoon tied to a stick.

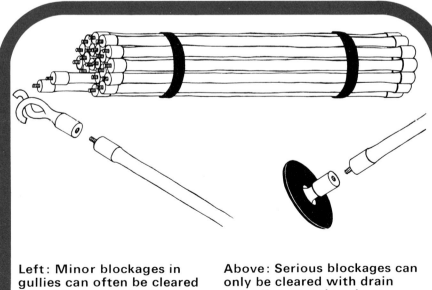

Above: Serious blockages can only be cleared with drain rods. Keep turning them clockwise in use to avoid a section disconnecting in the drain itself.

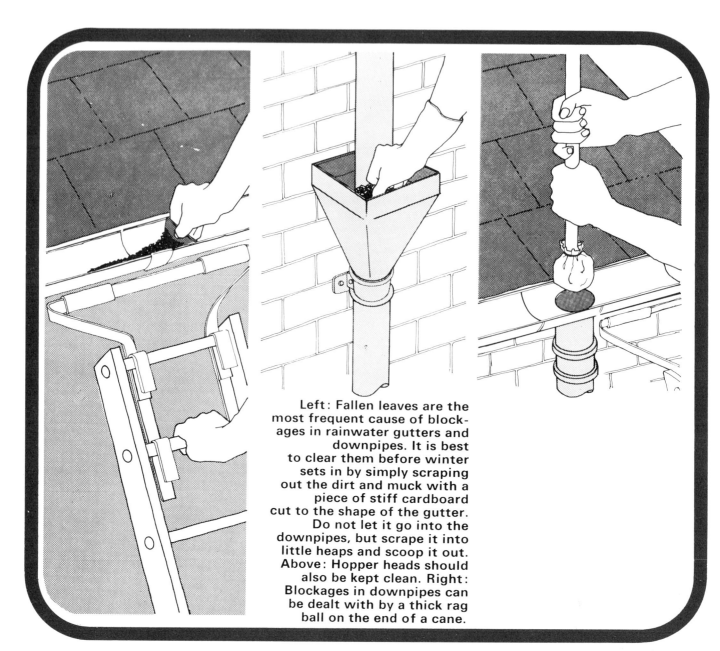

Left: Fallen leaves are the most frequent cause of blockages in rainwater gutters and downpipes. It is best to clear them before winter sets in by simply scraping out the dirt and muck with a piece of stiff cardboard cut to the shape of the gutter. Do not let it go into the downpipes, but scrape it into little heaps and scoop it out. **Above:** Hopper heads should also be kept clean. **Right:** Blockages in downpipes can be dealt with by a thick rag ball on the end of a cane.

is in the pipes between the manhole and the house; if the *chamber is full* of waste water, the blockage is further down the drainage system.

Tools
Never use improvised tools to try and clear away a blockage in a drain pipe — you may increase the problem tenfold by getting your tool stuck in the pipe. The best means of do-it-yourself drain clearance is to connect the garden hose and turn the water on to full pressure, adjust the nozzle to get as strong a jet as possible, then insert the hose into the blocked pipe. With luck, the force of the water will break down the blockage.

If you are a very independent sort of person, and not squeamish about mucky drains, you can hire a set of drain rods to clear away blockages. These are simple to use — merely push the rods up the drain, screwing on more lengths as you need them. One thing to remember, however, is to keep turning the rods *clockwise*

to ensure that they stay connected. If you turn them counter-clockwise by mistake, half of the rods will be left behind in the drain which will not help the blockage and will not please the hire shop.

Gutters
Gutters and rainwater pipes are most likely to get blocked in the autumn — by leaves. If during heavy rain the gutters begin to overflow, you should be able to clear the blockage yourself, providing that you can get up to the gutters. See if you can manage on a ladder (be sure it is firmly secured at ground level), or perhaps you can reach them from a dormer window?

All you need to do is scrape the gutters clear of all debris — let it fall over the edge to the ground below, rather than go down the rainwater pipe.

If the blockage is in the pipe, tie a rag to the end of a cane and ram it down the pipe until it clears and the rainwater runs freely again.

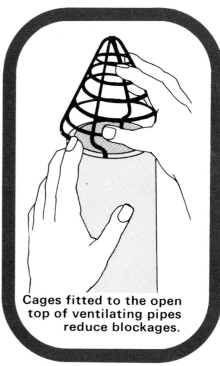

Cages fitted to the open top of ventilating pipes reduce blockages.

HOW CENTRAL HEATING WORKS

Below: A typical small bore hot-water central heating system. There are two separate circuits, one supplies the radiators and the other the taps. Hot water for radiators is drawn from the top of the boiler and circulated with the aid of a pump. The hot water taps are supplied by a heat exchanger unit in the hot water tank.

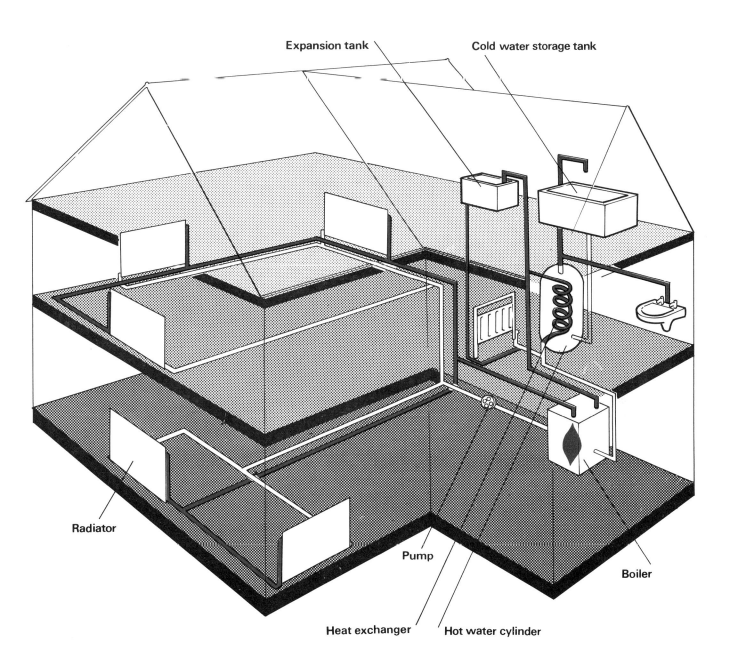

Expansion tank

Cold water storage tank

Radiator

Pump

Boiler

Heat exchanger

Hot water cylinder

Hot water radiators

In this system water, supplied from a special *feed tank*, is heated by a boiler and then circulated around two separate circuits. One circuit has all the radiators attached to it and the other sends hot water to a cylinder containing a *heat exchanger* which warms up water for the taps.

Older installations have thick pipes and work on a gravity principle — hot water rises naturally from the boiler and returns by force of gravity. Most newer systems have much thinner pipes (called 'small-bore' pipes) with a pump fitted to force the water around the system.

The heat output is normally controlled by thermostats which automatically turn the boiler off when the temperature has reached a certain level and switch it back on again when it drops below that level.

Boilers can be fired by gas, oil or solid fuel. With *gas boilers*, the supply is automatically switched on by a time switch and ignited by a pilot light. *This pilot should never be extinguished*, but if it does go out accidentally the supply is automatically cut off to avoid any accidents.

Solid-fuel boilers are normally fed by a hopper — a funnel-shaped container which pours anthracite on top of the fire at regular intervals as it is needed. Hoppers need filling about once a day in winter and once every two or three days in summer.

Oil-fired boilers are connected to a fuel tank, normally installed outdoors where it is unobtrusive yet accessible to the tanker lorries which will keep it supplied.

Maintenance of central heating systems should only be carried out by qualified engineers — never attempt to adjust any of the control mechanisms (except those illustrated in the following pages) and have the system overhauled every year in the autumn.

Warm air systems

Instead of sending hot water around the house to warm up radiators, this system distributes hot air around the house through ducts which lead to little grills set into the walls or floors. The air is pushed through the ducts by a fan and is either heated by a boiler (like those used in radiator systems, except that the water is replaced by air) or by electricity, usually operated at off-peak hours for cheaper rates.

Electric storage radiators

Storage radiators store up heat during the night (when electricity is normally cheaper because the demand is much less) and let it out slowly during the day. They need to be rather large in order to store up sufficient heat (normally in a material like fireclay or concrete).

Some storage radiators are fitted with fans which make them easier to control. They normally have much more insulation around them and

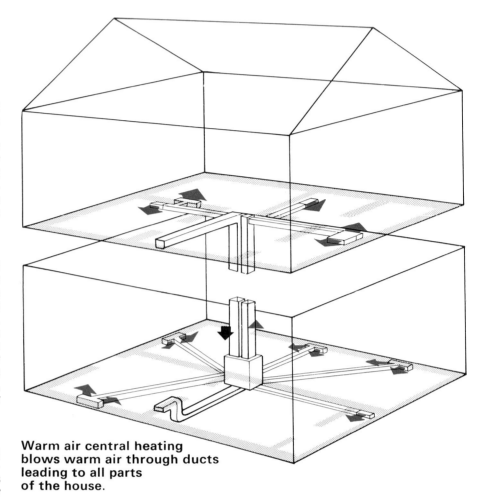

Warm air central heating blows warm air through ducts leading to all parts of the house.

give off comparatively little heat until the fan is switched on (often by a thermostat).

Underfloor heating

This type of system comprises heating elements (normally powered by off-peak electricity) laid in the concrete of solid floors. The floor, acting like a huge storage radiator, builds up heat during the off-peak supply hours and gives it out gradually throughout the day and night. Nice if you suffer from cold feet.

Underfloor heating comprises electric elements in solid floors.

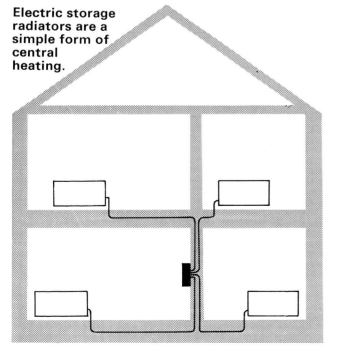

Electric storage radiators are a simple form of central heating.

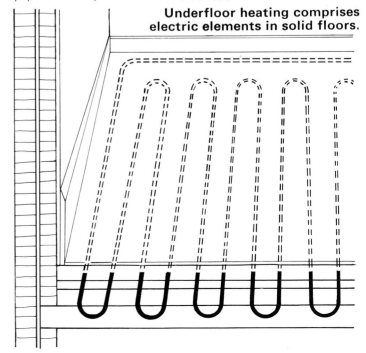

HOW TO KEEP CENTRAL HEATING IN PRIME CONDITION

All central heating systems should be serviced at least once a year by qualified engineers. Maintenance contracts, arranged directly with the fuel supplier, are normally the cheapest and most reliable ways of ensuring regular, efficient maintenance.

Ways to save

The way in which you use central heating can have a drastic effect upon both its efficiency and its reliability. Many of the measures you might be tempted to adopt to reduce running costs can prove to be false economy. In very cold weather, for example, *do not* shut off the system completely at night. It will take a long time to reach its operating temperature the following morning and, in fact, use more fuel for this effort than it would if it had been kept on — but turned down low — throughout the night.

Turn the thermostats down to about 10°C (50°F) when you go to bed — this will keep the system operating at minimal cost and enable it to warm up very quickly the following morning. It will also reduce condensation and eliminate the risk of possible frost damage.

Whether you are using the boiler for hot water only (during the summer) or for the central heating as well, do not turn the boiler thermostat down too low — with *small-bore systems* a setting of 82°C (180°F) is normal.

Obviously if you keep all the windows open, your running costs are going to be greatly increased because the system will be constantly battling to reach the required temperature. If you need to air a room, open the windows for a short time only and close the door to prevent loss of heat from other rooms in the house.

Room thermostats

Room thermostats control the circulating pump which forces water through the system. As the air in the room reaches the required temperature, the thermostat turns the pump off. With no water circulating, all the radiators will begin to cool until the temperature in the particular room

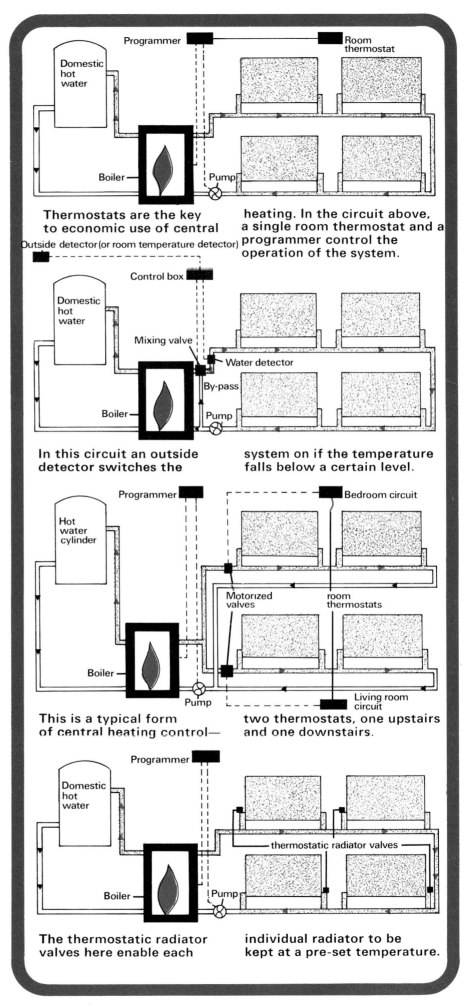

Thermostats are the key to economic use of central heating. In the circuit above, a single room thermostat and a programmer control the operation of the system.

In this circuit an outside detector switches the system on if the temperature falls below a certain level.

This is a typical form of central heating control— two thermostats, one upstairs and one downstairs.

The thermostatic radiator valves here enable each individual radiator to be kept at a pre-set temperature.

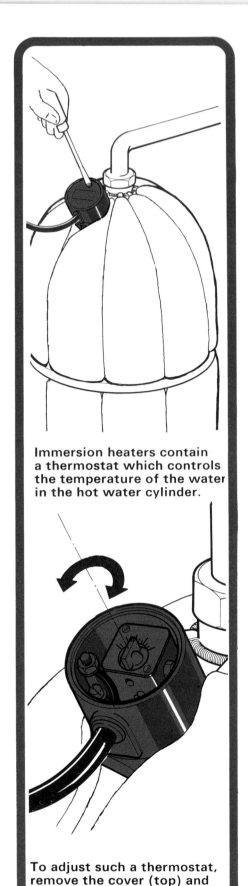

Immersion heaters contain a thermostat which controls the temperature of the water in the hot water cylinder.

To adjust such a thermostat, remove the cover (top) and turn the regulator screw to required temperature (above).

rest of the house. The extra warmth will cause the thermostat to reach the temperature at which it is set, prematurely, and shut off the circulating pump. You might then find that while you have one nice, cosy room, the other rooms in the house will be freezing.

Many people complain that central heating (particularly a warm-air system) causes dry throats or headaches. It certainly can happen, but the problem can be minimized by keeping the temperature as constant as possible and raising the humidity. Proprietary humidifiers range from simple clay jars of water which you hang on the radiators, to fancy electric appliances which discharge moistened air into the room. A more attractive remedy is to keep pot plants standing on stones in water-filled trays.

A GUIDE TO THE CONTROLS

Time clocks determine the hours during which the whole heating system will operate. Most time clocks allow for the system to be switched on and off twice during the day. A family out of the house for much of the day would probably set the time clock so that the system works in the mornings and evenings only.

Time clocks should make it possible for central heating to adapt to your particular needs — rather than the other way around. Some installations have an *electric programmer* instead of a time clock, and with these you can set up independent operating 'programmes' for heating and hot water.

Thermostats. The first thermostat in a central heating system is *attached to the boiler* and controls the maximum temperature of the water or the air which is being heated.

Room thermostats, normally fixed on the wall in the living room, control the temperature *of that room* — not necessarily the complete system. However, if no extra heating is used (see above), when the living room reaches a comfortable temperature of, say, 21°C (70°F), all the other rooms in the house should also be comfortably warm.

Radiator thermostats are sometimes used instead of the more usual valves. They control the flow of hot water through the radiator and enable the temperature of individual radiators to be maintained at any level.

Immersion heaters are necessary when the central heating system does not provide hot water at the sink, bath and basin. They, too, are controlled by a thermostat which governs the maximum temperature of the water.

To adjust an immersion thermostat, you must undo the screw holding the cover, remove the cover and, with a screwdriver, turn the regulator screw to the temperature required.

Radiator valves control the flow of water through the radiator. Turned off (clockwise), they isolate the radiator from the circulating hot water so that it quickly becomes cold.

Although you cannot make accurate temperature adjustments with a radiator valve, you can reduce the warmth of a radiator by partially closing the valve.

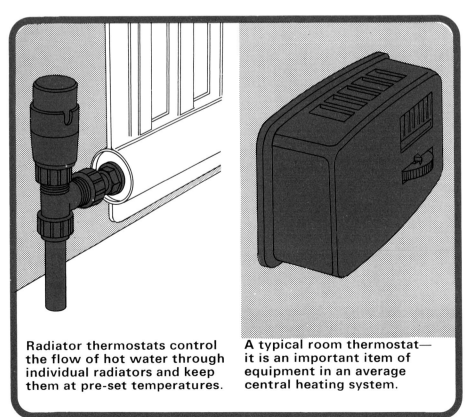

Radiator thermostats control the flow of hot water through individual radiators and keep them at pre-set temperatures.

A typical room thermostat— it is an important item of equipment in an average central heating system.

drops below the level at which the thermostat has been set. When that happens, the pump will start up again.

Remember, if you are using extra heating in the room with the thermostat (perhaps an open fire or a fan heater) it will affect the heating in the

CENTRAL HEATING: MAINTENANCE AND REPAIRS

Radiators — air locks

Air locks are the most common problem with radiators. You will know when you get one — the top of the radiator remains cold (because there is no water there) even when the bottom is scalding. On the side of the radiator, near the top, there is an air vent which can be turned with a special key. (Keys should have been supplied with the installation; if they have been lost, you can always buy them at an ironmonger). As you turn the key *anti-clockwise*, you will hear the air hissing out. Wait until water starts to trickle out instead of air, then quickly close the valve tightly.

Even if your central heating seems to be working perfectly well, it is a worthwhile precaution to 'bleed' the radiators of air at least once or twice during the winter.

If you find that you are constantly getting air locks in certain radiators, you can cure the problem permanently by fitting an automatic 'air eliminator' — a special valve which allows air to escape but retains water. This valve simply screws into the radiator in place of the air vent, but you will have to drain the radiator involved before you can make the swap.

Leaks from radiator joints can often be cured by gently tightening the relevant nut with an adjustable spanner.

Draining a central heating system

Switch off the boiler and the electric immersion heater if you have one; allow the system to cool for an hour or two. Shut off the water supply to the boiler either by closing the stop valve on the pipe leading into the expansion tank or by tying up the ball valve so that it does not rest in the tank.

You will find the 'drain cock' on the lowest pipe entering the boiler. Push a length of hosepipe on to the nozzle that protrudes out from the pipe and run it to the nearest outside drain. Open the drain cock by turning a little nut underneath (clockwise) with an adjustable spanner. Do not forget to close the drain cock before you start filling the system again.

If you plan to be away from home and intend to shut off the boiler completely, you should always drain your central heating system. It is, however, safer and less trouble to leave the system on, turned down very low.

If the system suddenly springs a bad leak, you should drain it as quickly as possible, rather than wait for a plumber to arrive. ALWAYS TURN THE BOILER OFF BEFORE DRAINING THE CENTRAL HEATING.

Noises: Radiators

Some radiators creak when the heating is switched on and off: the noise is caused by rapid expansion and contraction of the steel as it heats and cools. You can reduce creaking by adjusting the controls so that the

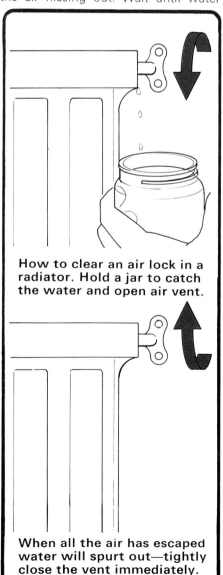

How to clear an air lock in a radiator. Hold a jar to catch the water and open air vent.

When all the air has escaped water will spurt out—tightly close the vent immediately.

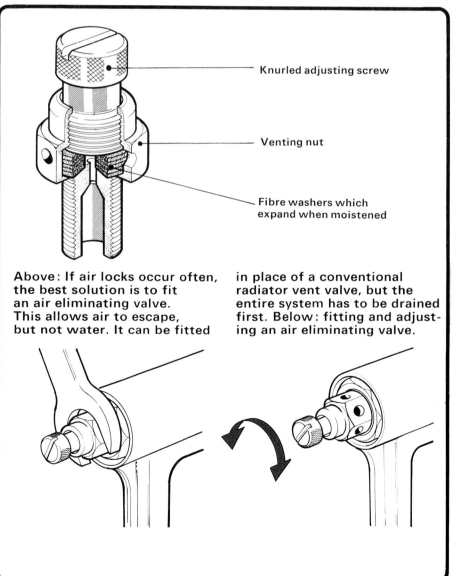

Knurled adjusting screw

Venting nut

Fibre washers which expand when moistened

Above: If air locks occur often, the best solution is to fit an air eliminating valve. This allows air to escape, but not water. It can be fitted in place of a conventional radiator vent valve, but the entire system has to be drained first. Below: fitting and adjusting an air eliminating valve.

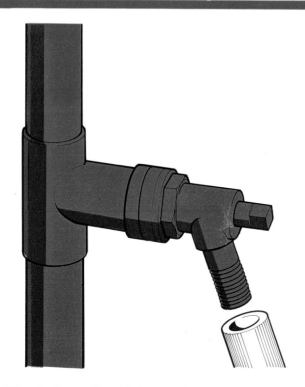

The drain cock which empties a central heating system is always on the lowest pipe entering the boiler.

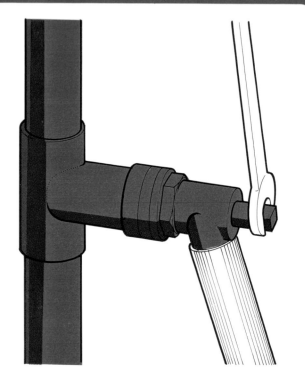

Fix a length of hose to the nozzle and run it to an outside drain, then open the nut under the drain cock with a spanner.

radiators remain switched on for longer periods, instead of constantly heating up and cooling down. Do this by turning the boiler thermostat down.

Alternatively, the metal radiator brackets can be replaced with special brackets which have a nylon-bearing surface.

Nasty hissing and knocking noises, which come from your central heating system when it is switched on full, normally indicates either that the pipes have become scaled up from hard water deposits, or that the water is overheating.

Hard water scaling in central heating is dangerous because it reduces the interior size of the pipes. The system becomes less and less efficient and could, eventually, explode.

If you find that you have bad scaling deposits inside your kettle, you can quite safely assume that you will get them inside your central heating system. A 'de-scaling capsule' (available at most hardware shops), which you hang inside the cold water storage tank in the attic, helps reduce the problem. But, if you have very bad scaling, you should call in expert help.

Some central heating authorities maintain that conventional heating systems will not become scaled up unless the water in the system is constantly being replaced or unless you have a 'direct' hot water system.

Overheating

Overheating can be caused by a boiler thermostat not working properly, failure of the pump, perhaps a blocked flue, or a jammed ball valve in the expansion tank which, thereby, does not allow enough water into the system.

Check the thermostat by turning it up and down — if you cannot hear a little click, it may be wrong. No click will be noticed on a solid fuel heating installation.

If the pump is running but the water is not circulating, it's probably due to an air-lock. At the top of the pump you will find a vent valve, operated either by a key or a screw-driver. Open the valve to bleed the air off and close it when water starts to dribble out, but be sure to switch the pump off before doing this.

Check the flue for obstructions, if you can. And finally, make sure that the ball valve in the expansion tank (the smaller of the two in the attic) is working. As it is used less frequently than the ball valve in the cold water tank, it's more liable to get stuck. If it does, it is usually possible to repair it. Page 27, **Repairing an overflow**, suggests several ways to repair ball valves. Study them carefully before doing anything.

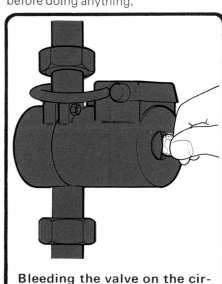

Bleeding the valve on the circulating pump.

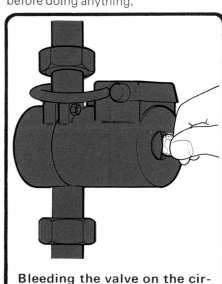

Reduce hard water scaling with a de-scaling capsule.

OIL HEATERS

Oil heaters are very efficient, inexpensive to run, and simple to maintain. But they are also potentially very dangerous — particularly older models. If an old paraffin heater is accidentally knocked over, it is easy for the fuel to pour out, and within seconds the whole room could be a sheet of flame.

In Britain, new models, approved by the British Standards Institution and bearing their famous 'kite' mark, have safety devices to prevent this from happening. Nevertheless, the ultimate responsibility for safety is on the user.

If it is possible and convenient to fix oil heaters in a stable position (many now have bolts or brackets for attaching to a wall or floor) you should do so. If it cannot be permanently fixed, *never* move it while it is alight. Never stand it in a draught, and never leave it where it is liable to be knocked or tipped over.

Remember, finally, that oil heaters produce a great deal of condensation. It is not a good idea to use them in rooms without reasonable ventilation.

Convector heaters

Oil convector heaters have wicks which soak up the paraffin oil and burn with a blue flame. The heated air is pushed upwards and outwards by cold air as it is drawn in underneath to be heated.

To get the best results from oil heaters they should always be kept clean. The only other maintenance needed is to trim or replace the wick as necessary.

Most convector heaters can be taken to pieces by hand for cleaning purposes. Those parts that can be detached should be brushed clean, washed in soapy water and dried thoroughly.

If a wick becomes contaminated either with oil, petrol or water, it will not burn properly and will need to be replaced. If the source of the contamination is in the fuel container, empty it and clean it with a dry rag before re-filling. Pour old paraffin oil into the ground — it is illegal to tip it down the drain.

When replacing a wick, make sure you have the right type and size for your particular model of heater. There are many variations, so always tell the shop the make and model of your heater when you are buying a new one.

Paraffin heaters work best if the wick is frequently trimmed of carbon deposits around its edge. Most heaters have a special 'wick trimmer' attached to the casing. All you need to

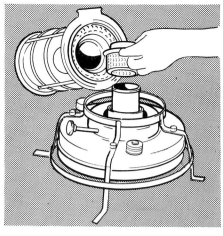

To replace a wick on an Aladdin heater, remove the chimney and the burner. Unscrew the top with a quarter turn clockwise.

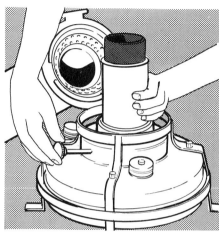

Turn up the wick and carrier until it frees itself from the carrier guide.

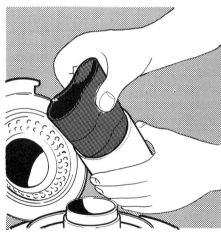

Remove the wick by squeezing it and sliding it out of the carrier.

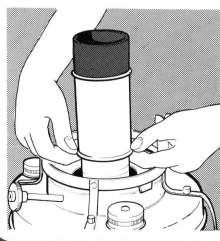

The new wick may then be positioned and the carrier and chimney reassembled.

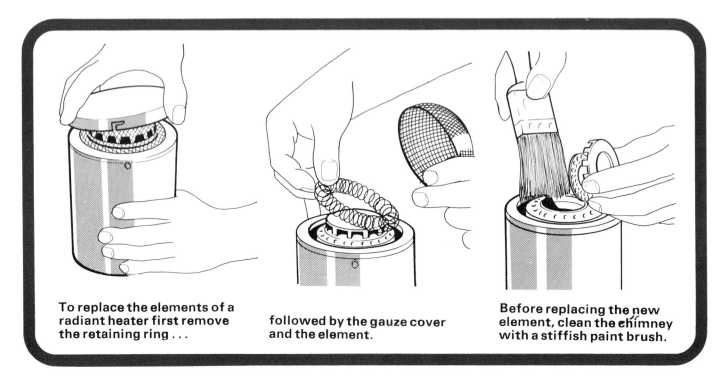

To replace the elements of a radiant heater first remove the retaining ring . . .

followed by the gauze cover and the element.

Before replacing the new element, clean the chimney with a stiffish paint brush.

do is lay the trimmer on the burner and turn up the wick until it can be seen through the slots in the trimmer. Revolve the trimmer until the wick is even and free of carbon and then wipe the trimmer clean, replace it and readjust the wick.

To replace an Aladdin wick, remove the chimney and unscrew the nuts holding the burner on to the base of the heater. Remove the burner unit and unscrew the top with a quarter turn anti-clockwise. Turn up the wick until the winder cogs disengage from

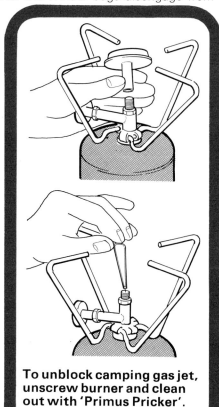

To unblock camping gas jet, unscrew burner and clean out with 'Primus Pricker'.

the wick holder and pull it out (you may have to cut it to get it free). Hold the winder out and slide the ends of the new wick into the gap between the winder and the centre tube. Pull the ends from underneath until the wick fits snugly over the tube. Refit the wick holder and wind the wick down to an appropriate height. Then replace the burner and chimney.

To replace a Valor wick, remove the chimney and lift the flame spreader from the centre tube. Unscrew the base of the chimney and lift it off, then turn up the wick until the ratchet is free from the winder. Pull the old wick off the tube and replace it with a new one, making sure the ratchet faces the winder. When the winder cogs are engaged in the ratchet, wind the wick down to the right level and refit the chimney base, flame spreader and chimney.

Radiant heaters

Radiant heaters work on a different principle to the more conventional convector heaters. The wick heats a gauze dome which glows red and radiates heat from a reflecting bowl. The fuel is fed to the burner by a drip system which can be controlled to increase or decrease the heat output.

If a radiant heater smokes it means that the wick needs replacing, or that the fuel supply is too fast and the control valve must be adjusted. If the wire gauze glows only in patches or gets coated with soot, replace the spiral element just underneath the gauze.

Radiant heaters should be stripped and cleaned once a year.

Pressure heaters

Pressure heaters and lamps do ·not actually burn paraffin oil, but rather

the vapour that paraffin gives off under pressure. They are very economical but not as easy to adjust as other paraffin heaters, and they make a faint hissing noise when alight. All pressure heaters and lamps can be taken apart by hand; the only maintenance they need is an annual cleaning and overhaul. The 'vaporizer' (the tube that leads to the mantle) tends to get clogged with carbon deposits after considerable use and so may require replacing every now and again.

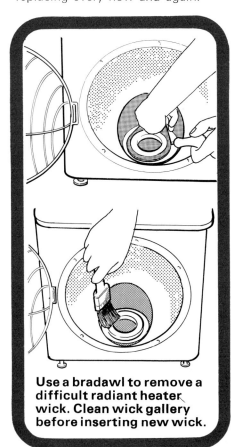

Use a bradawl to remove a difficult radiant heater wick. Clean wick gallery before inserting new wick.

EASY REPAIRS FOR DECORATIONS

In an average family home, 12 months wear and tear on the painting and surface decorations shows. Yet it is ridiculous to expect to redecorate the entire house every year. To keep your decorations looking smart, they need timely repairs. Here are some easy short cuts.

REPAIR MATERIALS—FILLERS AND SEALERS

Filling gaps, cracks, dents and holes requires, appropriately enough, a filler. So far, very easy. The difficult question is, which filler? Different types are offered on the market and the simplest way to find out which one to use is to ask your local handyman's shop to recommend the right ingredient for the job you want to do.

For those who treasure their independence, however, the following is a quick guide to quick fillers:

Cellulose filler (i.e. Polyfilla) is available ready-mixed in tubes or in powder form, which must be mixed with water into a stiff paste. Use it (or a similar product) for all small cracks and holes in plaster and woodwork that is to be decorated.

Mastic-type fillers are flexible and should be used to stop up gaps where movement is likely to occur between the two sides — between walls and door or window frames, for example. Slamming doors would crack rigid filling materials like putty or Polyfilla.

Plastic wood is available in different shades to match the colour of unpainted woodwork, but don't expect miracles. Use it for holes and cracks in all bare, unpolished, woodwork.

Beeswax is an old-fashioned filler, but still a useful one because you can colour it yourself with vegetable dye and mix a perfect match to any colour timber. It requires patience, however, because you have to melt the 'beeswax and keep adding dye until you have exactly the right colour. Use it for chipped or damaged, polished wood that matters.

Epoxy-resin adhesive will fill cracks or chips in marble fireplace surrounds. It, too, can be coloured with vegetable dye to match the colour of the damaged marble.

Liquid sealers are used to cover over whatever substance is already on the surface of walls or woodwork and

seal it in so that other decoration can be applied over it. You need them, for example, to stop oily stains seeping through paint onto woodwork, or to stabilize old, powdery distemper so that it can be painted over.

APPLYING THE REMEDIES—TO RENDERING, WOOD, PLASTER

Efflorescence is the feathery white powder that often appears on new brickwork or plaster. It is caused by water drying out of the walls and drawing soluble salts to the surface. It cannot damage exterior brickwork, but it can spoil interior decorations.

Outside you can eliminate it by brushing the walls occasionally with a stiff broom. Inside, brush away the powder and any other loose material, then paint a 'neutralizing liquid' (get it at any handyman's shop) over the affected part. Apply two or three coats at half hour intervals, then leave to dry for at least 24 hours before patching up the decorations.

Knot stains first appear through painted woodwork as little pale brown smudges. If they are left they become large, dark brown blobs; on light-coloured paintwork they look most disfiguring. They are caused by the oily resin in the wood knot seeping through the paint. Of course, the knots should have been treated before the wood was used, but very often they are not.

The only permanent remedy is to

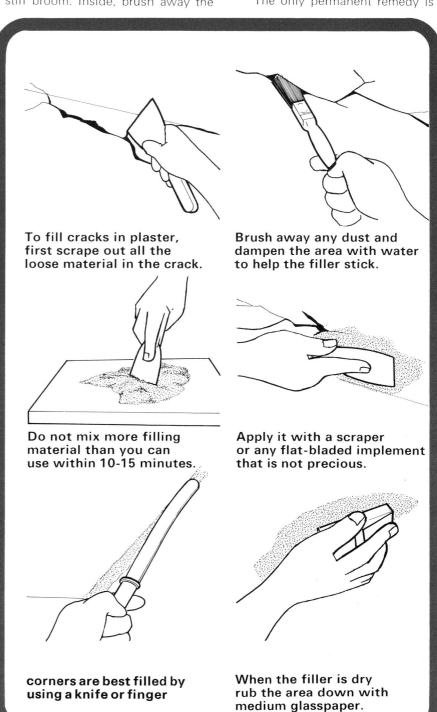

To fill cracks in plaster, first scrape out all the loose material in the crack.

Brush away any dust and dampen the area with water to help the filler stick.

Do not mix more filling material than you can use within 10-15 minutes.

Apply it with a scraper or any flat-bladed implement that is not precious.

corners are best filled by using a knife or finger

When the filler is dry rub the area down with medium glasspaper.

strip off the paint around the stain (use a proprietary paint stripper and scraper). When you reach bare wood, scrape off any resin from the knot and rub down the patch with glass paper to clean it completely. Apply two coats of knot sealer (buy the smallest bottle you can — it is not expensive but you will need only the tiniest amount), then patch up the painted area.

The same remedy can be applied to any oil or grease stain coming through paintwork, although you may need a different kind of sealer.

Small holes or cracks in plaster are very easy to patch up. First rake out all loose plaster inside and around the hole. If you are using a powder filler, mix it into a good stiff paste. Do not make up too much because you cannot keep it — it will go rock hard within half an hour or so. A 'stripping knife' is the best tool to apply the filler with, but if you do not have one, an ordinary kitchen knife with a straight edge will work.

Brush away any dust around the hole or crack and then dampen the hole slightly; this will help the filler to stick. Press in the filler with the knife and smooth the final layer as flat as you can — do not worry if it is not perfect, when it is dry you can sandpaper it absolutely flat with medium to fine glasspaper.

If filling bigger holes or cracks, it is easiest to do it in stages, allowing each layer to dry before applying the next. Clean all tools immediately.

PAINTWORK

Dents and chips in painted woodwork can be concealed by filling them with a cellulose filler and painting over. Even if the chip in the paintwork is only as thick as one or two coats of paint, it is worth filling it properly — no matter how many times you paint over an unfilled chip, you will always be able to see it.

First sandpaper the dent or chip with medium to fine glasspaper to provide a good key. Then, fill the hole and smooth it over carefully with a flat edge so that it is flush with the surface of the woodwork. When the filler is dry, sandpaper it lightly with fine glasspaper until it is completely smooth. Paint over the surface, 'feathering' the top coat outwards to hide the edges of the repair. Feathering is done by working from the centre of the repaired area with brush strokes that lift gently off the paintwork at the edges (see Page 45, bottom).

Blisters in paintwork are caused either by moisture or resin which is trapped under the surface and is trying to break through, or by heat — window ledges in full sunlight all day often suffer from blisters. To repair these, first cut out the blistered paint only with a knife. If the cause is moisture

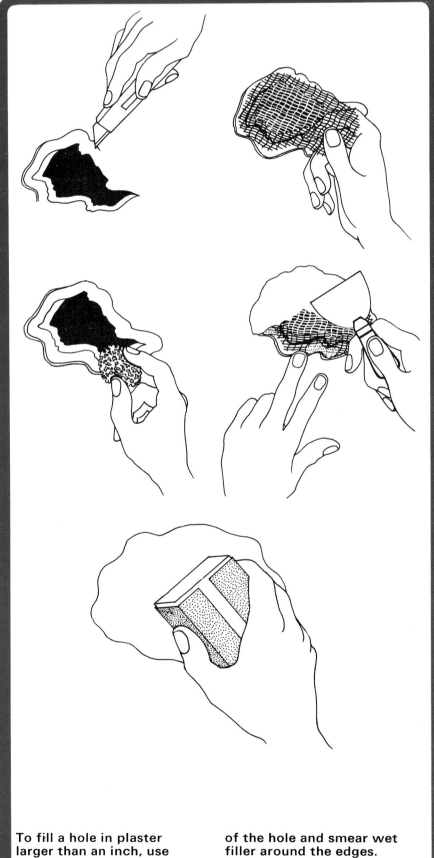

To fill a hole in plaster larger than an inch, use 'scrim cloth' to provide a key. First cut away the surface plaster around the hole and cut a layer or two of 'scrim' to cover the area. Damp the surround of the hole and smear wet filler around the edges. Press the scrim cloth on to the filler while it is still wet and cover it with a thin coat of filler. Apply further coats if necessary and smooth it with glasspaper.

or resin, treat the wood with a sealer before filling and repainting. If the cause is heat, there may not be much you can do about it, except repaint the area every now and again. Either way, rub down the blistered area with glasspaper until it is smooth. If there is still a hole, fill it, then repaint.

Touching up paintwork can do more harm than good unless it is done properly. First, most paint colours start to fade after a few months (no matter what the manufacturers may claim). White is the worst offender — it takes on a distinctly yellow tinge after a short while. So touching up year-old paintwork with fresh paint often leaves patches more conspicuous than any marks you may be trying to hide.

The answer to this difficulty? Paint the whole length of that particular piece of woodwork — better, for example, that a window sill should be a slightly different shade than the rest of the window, than for it to have patches of different colour paint all over it.

If colour is not a problem, take care that you do not give the game away by bad painting. To disguise touched-up paintwork, always 'feather' the top coat outwards to hide the edges.

Dents and chips in polished woodwork can rarely be completely hidden by plastic wood; The colour probably will not be exactly right, and furthermore, the texture of plastic wood is not like real wood.

More precise repairs can be made with melted beeswax, coloured with vegetable dye to match the wood. You can get both from your local builders' merchant. Break up the beeswax into small pieces and melt it slowly over a low heat on the stove, but take care when melting the wax as it gives off a flammable explosive gas. When it is liquid begin adding the dye, mixing it in slowly until the colour is right. Leave the wax to set. When it is hard, prise it out of the tin and work it in your fingers until it is malleable, like modelling compound. Press it into the dent or chip with the warmed handle of a spoon; slightly overfill the hole to allow for shrinkage.

When it has cooled you will be able to shave it smooth with a sharp knife or single-sided razor blade. Gently rub the edges with finest glasspaper. Finally, polish the repaired area with the same polish you would normally use on the wood.

WALLPAPER

Peeling wallpaper should be stuck back into place as soon as it is noticed. Children find it highly difficult to resist the temptation to pull at peeling wallpaper, so what starts as a two-minute repair job could easily end up as a major re-decoration project.

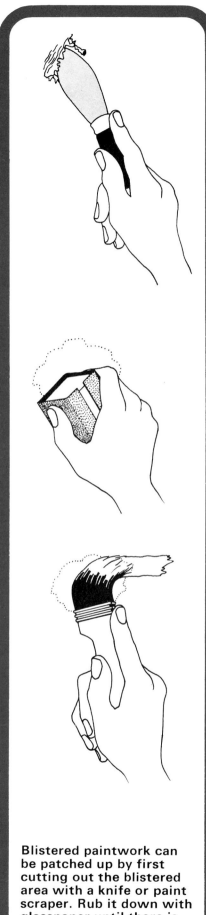

Blistered paintwork can be patched up by first cutting out the blistered area with a knife or paint scraper. Rub it down with glasspaper until there is no ridge and then carefully re-paint, feathering the brush strokes at the edges.

Almost any glue will do the trick, but you will probably find a rubber-based adhesive, such as Cow Gum, will work best because any excess can be neatly cleaned away. Lift up the peeling edge, applying the glue *thinly* and simply press the edge back. Wipe away any excess adhesive. If you have a little roller of any kind to run along the seams it will help make a neater job.

Beware of handling papers with a delicate finish (i.e. many French ones) as any glue on the surface will ruin them.

Blistered wallpaper can be dealt with in two ways. If you happen to have a syringe in the house, you can fill it with wallpaper paste, jab the blister, inject some paste into it, then press the blister flat so that it sticks.

A less esoteric remedy, and generally more successful, is to make two diagonal cuts across the blister, fold back and paste the four triangular flaps, then stick them back onto the wall. If you roll the seams lightly, the cuts will not be noticeable.

Patching torn wallpaper is easy, provided that the wall covering is a paper that you can tear with your hands and you have some extra wallpaper. First, tear away the damaged and loose paper, leaving the edges 'feathered' (see below). Cut a piece of paper larger than the hole, and match the pattern, if necessary. Then tear the edges of the patch all the way around so that the layered edge is on the back of the paper (see page 46). Apply paste to the patch and stick it over the hole, making sure you have matched the pattern exactly. Roll or press the feathered edges down and you should hardly be able to see the repair.

If the wall covering is vinyl or hessian and cannot be torn, patching is trickier. The best way to do it is to cut a replacement piece bigger than the torn area, hold it up against the wall and match the pattern. Then, holding the patch so that it overlaps evenly over the hole, cut a neat square patch with a sharp knife through *both* layers of wallpaper (see page 46). Be absolutely certain that you hold the patch securely in place; if it slips the patch will not fit properly.

Remove the square from the wall and discard the outside of the patch, which should now fit the hole in the wall covering exactly. Fix it in place with wallpaper paste.

Stains on ordinary wallpaper can often be removed by simply washing them with a mild detergent and water. But, always check first to see that the pattern is colourfast by trying a small piece in a dark corner. Work from the bottom upwards so that the paper does not get too wet before being washed.

There are a number of proprietary cleaning fluids that will remove grease spots on wallpaper. With aerosol cleaners, you spray the spot and leave it to dry. Then, lightly brush off the white powder residue. Fuller's earth mixed with a mineral turpentine substitute also makes a good cleaner on washable papers.

Greasy patches on vinyl can be removed by lubricating them with lard and then wiping them off carefully with a clean dry cloth.

CHIPPED MARBLE

Chips out of marble fireplaces can be made good by mixing an epoxy resin adhesive, such as Araldite, with powdered vegetable dye to match the colour of the marble. Use a spatula or springy kitchen knife to apply the resin to the chipped area and mould it into shape. You can file it down, if necessary, with a piece of Carborundum stone. The same piece of stone will remove light scratches from marble.

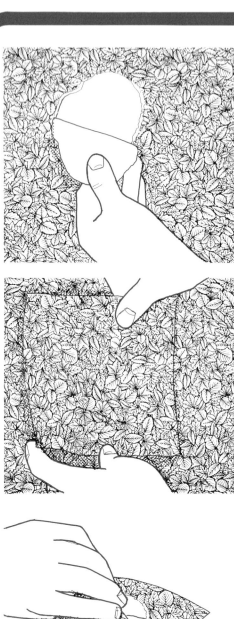

To patch torn wallpaper, first tear away the damaged area, leaving the edges of the paper 'feathered'.

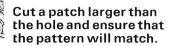

Cut a patch larger than the hole and ensure that the pattern will match.

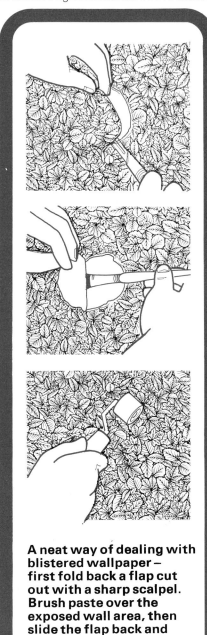

A neat way of dealing with blistered wallpaper – first fold back a flap cut out with a sharp scalpel. Brush paste over the exposed wall area, then slide the flap back and roll it flat.

Tear the edges of the patch all the way round leaving the layered edge on the back of the paper.

Stick the patch into position carefully and roll the edges until they are obscured.

FLOORS

How to stop rugs from slipping

Rugs which slip on polished floors are a menace. You can fix them permanently with large press-studs fastened all around the edge (one part nailed to the floor, the other sewn to the underside of the rug). But this is only satisfactory if the position of the rug is never going to be changed.

One of the simplest solutions is to buy a special non-slip underlay, but it is cheaper and just as effective to use $\frac{1}{4}$in. (6 mm) thick, foam plastic sheeting. Cut it about $\frac{1}{2}$in. (12 mm) smaller than the rug all around and fix it to the underside with a latex-based adhesive. This will prevent the rug from slipping, even on the shiniest surface.

Any woven carpets which are cut to fit should always be bound with carpet tape to keep the edges from fraying.

Curled edges

If a carpet begins to curl at the edges, it can be held in place with a proprietary metal strip. These are first tacked to the floor and the carpet is then slipped under its edge — spikes in the strip hold the carpet down.

If using such a strip, all carpet underlays must be trimmed away first, as they will not fit under the strip. Be very careful not to cut your carpet.

Patching carpets

Whenever you have a carpet fitted, always keep any remnants to use as patches if the need arises. The appearance of a carpet is spoiled if one part is badly worn, or burned or indelibly stained — a patch will not make it look like new again, but it will certainly make it look much better.

It is easier to make an accurate patch if you can turn back the carpet and cut out the damaged area from underneath. Mark a square around the damaged area with a ball point pen or chalk (make the square align with the weave of the carpet). In order to stop the edges from fraying, coat latex-based adhesive all around the square and rub it in before you cut out the square with a sharp knife.

Place the square and the remnant back to back (matching the pattern if possible), mark around it and cut out the replacement piece. Use hessian tape coated with latex adhesive to stick the patch in place. Fix the tape so that it covers the hole on the underside of the carpet first. Replace the carpet and press in the patch, also coated with adhesive. Be sure that the pile is lying in the right direction.

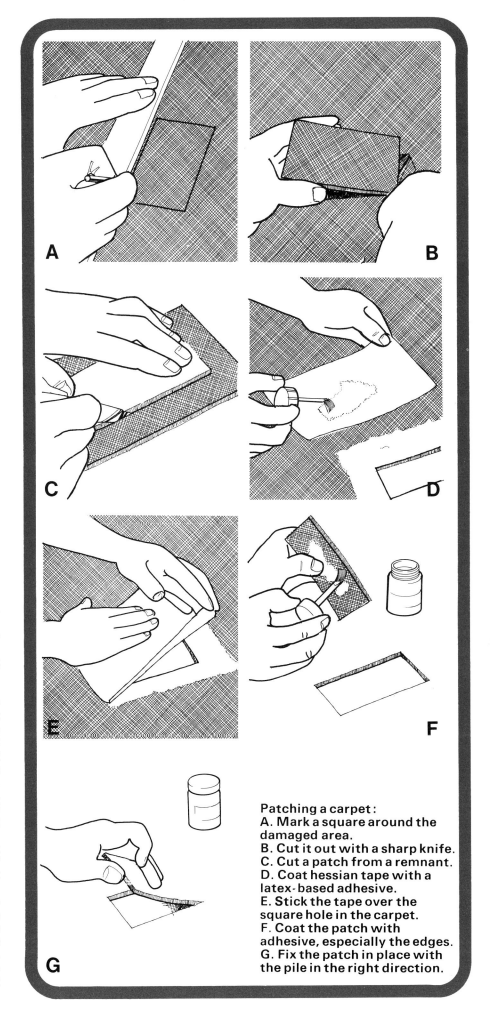

Patching a carpet:
A. Mark a square around the damaged area.
B. Cut it out with a sharp knife.
C. Cut a patch from a remnant.
D. Coat hessian tape with a latex-based adhesive.
E. Stick the tape over the square hole in the carpet.
F. Coat the patch with adhesive, especially the edges.
G. Fix the patch in place with the pile in the right direction.

If you are unable to lift the carpet up, cut a square patch from a remnant slightly bigger than the damaged area. Lay it over the damage with the pile and pattern matching and hold it in place temporarily with a couple of tacks.

Cut around the edge of the square through the carpet as accurately as you can. Pull out the tacks, remove the damaged square and make sure that the patch fits the area exactly. Cut strips of strong contact-adhesive tape slightly longer than the sides of the square patch. Lift each side of the carpet in turn and fix the tape underneath the edge so that there is an overlap all around. Press the patch into place and lightly hammer along the joins to ensure the tape is secured.

Patching pile rugs

Cigarette burns or small holes in woollen rugs can be repaired with 4-ply wool or special carpet wool in a matching colour. Trim off any singed or damaged tufts with a pair of small scissors, then dab a latex-based adhesive into the hole. Cut the wool into strips slightly longer than the pile of the rug until you have a bunch about the size of the hole. Cut the bunch off clean at one end and stand it in the adhesive, working in more strands if necessary.

When the adhesive has dried, cut the strands flush with the pile of the rug and tease the ends with a needle to blend in with the surrounding tufts.

Patching vinyl or linoleum coverings

The best way to cut an accurate patch for a linoleum or vinyl floor covering is to cut out the damaged area at the same time as you cut the patch.

Lay a remnant over the damage and match the pattern. Fix it in place with tacks or drawing pins to stop it from slipping. Then cut through *both* layers with a strong, sharp knife — either a special lino-cutter or handyman's knife. If it is an intricate pattern, the patch will probably be less obtrusive if its edges follow the lines of the pattern. If it is a plain colour, cut a square.

Lift out the damaged area and use a glue to fix the edges of the new patch into place. If it is easier, join the patch to the existing covering with a waterproof adhesive tape fixed around the edges on the underside.

Filling gaps in floorboards

Gaps between floorboards are unsightly and a source of draughts. They are caused by shrinkage of the boards after they have been laid. Probably the best repair to a badly gaping floor is made by lifting the floorboards and replacing them tightly together. However, this may be a much

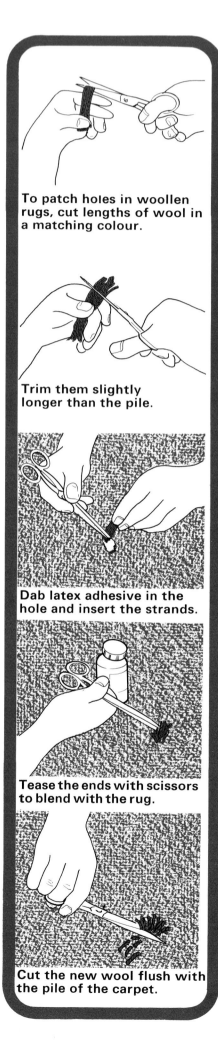

To patch holes in woollen rugs, cut lengths of wool in a matching colour.

Trim them slightly longer than the pile.

Dab latex adhesive in the hole and insert the strands.

Tease the ends with scissors to blend with the rug.

Cut the new wool flush with the pile of the carpet.

more involved task than you care to tackle. A simpler method is to fill small gaps with a proprietary wood stopping and sand smooth, or to use a home-made paper paste.

Make the paper paste by tearing waste paper into small strips and mixing it into a pulp by adding boiling water, a little at a time. When it is like a smooth paste, begin adding cellulose-based wallpaper paste, stirring all the time until the mixture is *very* thick.

Spread it into the gaps with a scraper or the broad blade of a knife, making sure it is pressed down well. Leave it to dry for two or three days and then rub it down with glasspaper (medium).

If the floor is going to be covered by a carpet or other covering, it does not matter what sort of paper you use. If, however, you want the gaps to be indistinguishable from the rest of the floor, use an unprinted paper, dyed with a proprietary liquid dye to match the colour of the floor.

Creaks

Creaking floorboards can sometimes be silenced by shaking French chalk or talcum powder into the gaps. This acts as a lubricant and stops the squeaking when the boards rub against each other. If this does not work, the only solution is to *screw* the boards down—they are normally held by nails and the creaking is caused because the nails do not grip the boards tightly enough.

Replacing floor tiles

Cracked or damaged floor tiles are easy to replace, regardless of whether they are plastic, cork or clay.

First, remove the damaged tile and all traces of the adhesive used to fix it. Always work from the centre outwards and avoid damaging adjacent tiles. With clay or quarry tiles, gently crack the whole surface with a hammer so that you can remove them bit by bit. Plastic and cork tiles may be laid on paper felt; if so, this too must be replaced.

Always use replacement tiles of the same make, size and colour, and check that they fit before trying to stick them down. Remember to allow for the thickness of the adhesive when you are checking the fit.

Different kinds of tiles need different adhesives. Always apply it according to the maker's instructions and after the replacement tile has been fixed in position, wipe the excess adhesive away immediately.

Do not lay new vinyl tiles on old, because an adhesive layer between the vinyls produces a chemical reaction which causes movement between the two layers. Old lino, vinyl sheeting or tiles should always be stripped off first.

FIXING AND FASTENING

Fixing things to walls

It's a great temptation, when you want to fix something to a wall, to simply pound in a nail here and there. Don't. Unless you are very, very lucky, nails will not secure anything to a wall safely.

The first thing you must ascertain is whether the wall is solid or hollow. If it is an interior wall it may be hollow (i.e. plaster fixed on each side of a thick wooden framework). Try tapping it at a couple of places — does it *sound* hollow?

If you cannot make up your mind, mark the position where you want the fixture and then try driving a screw in (use a bradawl to start the hole first). If it's a hollow wall you will suddenly notice that the screw is no longer 'biting' on anything — even when it is right in, it will still turn easily. If it's a solid wall, the screw will hold.

Having established that, all you need to do is choose the right fasteners to use . . . .

Solid walls

Solid walls are made of brick, concrete or aggregate building blocks. Screws or nails driven in directly tend to make the surrounding material crumble with the result that having driven in the screw or nail, you will probably find you can lift it straight out without any effort. Obviously, such a fixing is useless.

The way around the difficulty is to make a hole into which you can fit in a special plug. You then drive the screw into the plug, which expands and gets a tight grip on the surrounding masonry.

Wall plugs are normally made of fibre, plastic or nylon and they are often called by the trade name of Rawlplug. It is *important* that the size of the hole, plug and screw all correspond, so you might do best to use a packaged fixing kit which will include the tool to make the hole and corresponding plugs and screws.

To make a hole in a solid wall, first mark the exact spot where you want it to be by 'offering up' the object you want to fix to the wall. With a hammer, tap the point of the Rawldrill gently into the mark. It will go through the outer layer of plaster very quickly, but progress will be slower when you reach the masonry behind.

Turn the tool slightly after each blow with the hammer to ensure a neat hole and to stop it from jamming

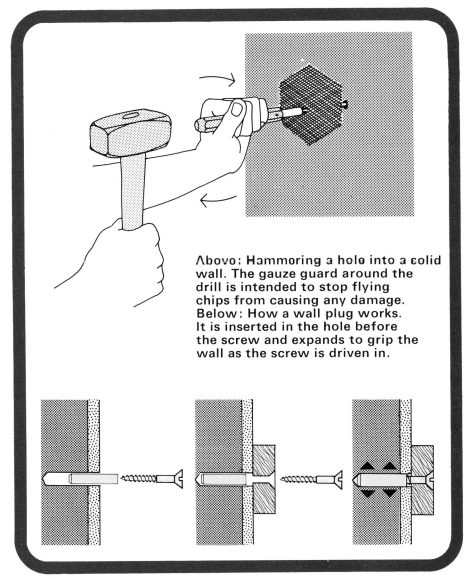

Above: Hammering a hole into a solid wall. The gauze guard around the drill is intended to stop flying chips from causing any damage. Below: How a wall plug works. It is inserted in the hole before the screw and expands to grip the wall as the screw is driven in.

tight in the wall. When the hole is deep enough (measure how much of the screw has to go into the wall and choose a plug of that length), clear away loose dust. Insert the tip of the screw into the end of the plug with a couple of turns and push the plug right into the hole.

Remove the screw (leaving the plug in the hole), push it through the fixing point of whatever you are hanging and then drive the screw into the plug until it is tight.

If the hole is really *too big* for the plug (it sometimes happens if the masonry is rather crumbly, that you cannot make a nice neat hole) do not just cross your fingers and hope it will work, because it will not. What you will need is a packet of composition filler such as Screwfix. This is a strange white fibre which becomes dough-like when it is moistened. All you have to do is mould it into a plastic consistency and then pack the hole with it, ramming it in hard, bit by bit.

When the cavity is full, pierce a hole for the screw. If you are putting up something very heavy, wait until the filler has dried out before driving in the screw. With most things, how-

ever, you can put the screw in straight away.

Hollow walls and ceilings

Hollow walls and ceilings need special kinds of fixings which provide support behind the panel when the screw is tightened. They all work on roughly the same principle: a gadget is fixed on the end of a bolt; this can then be slid through a small hole in the wall and when it is in the cavity it opens out.

The most common sorts of cavity fixings are gravity or spring 'toggles' — little metal bars which either drop or spring open behind the surface of the wall. Nylon or plastic 'anchors' are an alternative.

To attach a fixture to a hollow wall, you must first make a hole just large enough for the fixing gadget to be slipped through (see page 50). Do not test it by putting it right through, however, because you will not be able to get it out again!

Unscrew the toggle or anchor and slip the bolt through the object to be fixed. Replace the toggle or anchor on the end of the bolt, then push the bolt through the hole in the wall as far as it will go.

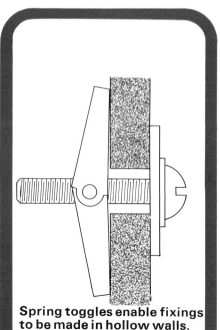

Spring toggles enable fixings to be made in hollow walls.

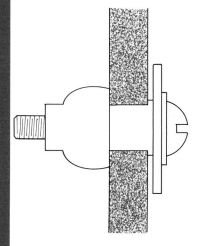

Rubber rawlnuts can be used in hollow and solid walls. The rubber sleeve expands when the bolt is tightened.

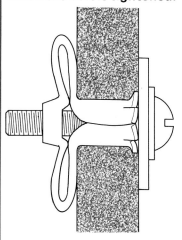

Collapsible anchors will remain in place if the bolt is removed.

Start tightening the bolt with a screwdriver and you will feel the toggle or anchor beginning to bite behind the panel. Screw it up until the fixture is held rigid against the wall.

Very heavy objects should not be hung on cavity walls with only toggle bolts or similar fixings to support them. If the stress is too great the object could pull the plasterboard from the wall. In this case fixing should be done by screwing directly into the wall's wooden framework, or 'studs'. You should be able to locate the position of the studs by tapping along the wall — when the hollow knocking turns to a dull thud, you will know there is a stud behind the plaster.

If you have no luck in doing this, make a series of trial holes in the plaster with a bradawl until you strike a stud. Most studs are either 12, 16 or 24 inches apart (305 mm, 407 mm, 610 mm).

So, having found one, you should not have much problem in locating the others.

If you are screwing directly into the wooden framework of a partition wall, there is no need to use wall plugs.

Nails for fixing

Picture hooks are the one exception to the rule not to pound nails directly into walls. Because they are very thin and sharp, because they are driven in at an angle and because the hook is held flat against the wall so that it takes a lot of strain, it is safe to use picture hooks in solid walls for most ordinary picture frames. But, if you are putting up something with an enormous gilt frame or a massive, modern work in steel, obviously, one little picture hook will not be enough.

What to do when wall fixtures fall down.

If a bathroom cupboard suddenly comes crashing down or a shelf falls away from the wall and deposits its contents in pieces on the floor, there is always a reason. Normally it is because it was not put up properly in the first place.

When the dust has cleared, first examine the holes left in the wall. It is likely that the screws will have ripped the old plugs out, so you will probably need to pack the holes with a composition filler of some sort before trying to replace the object. Make sure you force the filler well down into the holes to avoid a repetition of the disaster.

Do not use the same screws to fix the object back up again, and if they seem a little bit short, use new screws $\frac{1}{4}$in. (6 mm) longer.

If the crash has left truly enormous holes in the wall, it is safer to re-site the object, even if it is only by

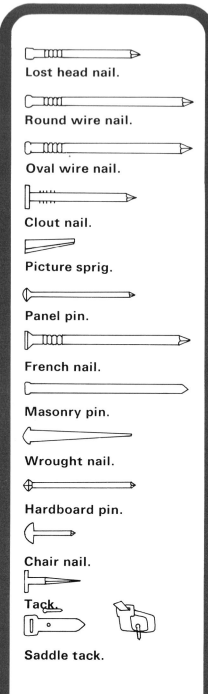

Lost head nail.

Round wire nail.

Oval wire nail.

Clout nail.

Picture sprig.

Panel pin.

French nail.

Masonry pin.

Wrought nail.

Hardboard pin.

Chair nail.

Tack.

Saddle tack.

Lost head nails can be punched below a surface. Round wire nails are stronger. Oval nails are unlikely to split wood. Clouts will fix felt or plasterboard, sprigs hold glass in frames. Panel pins are for small pieces of wood. French nails are for rough work. Masonry pins penetrate masonry, wrought nails can be bent over for extra grip. Hardboard pins sink into hardboard, chair nails are for upholstery. Tacks are for fixing carpets or fabric and saddle tacks hold wire.

a few inches, rather than risk it happening again. Fill the old holes with a cellulose-based filler, such as Poly-filla, and make new ones at least 3 in. (76 mm) away.

Nails

Although nails will not hold properly in walls they are useful for dozens of other repair jobs around the house. But you should always use the right nail for the right job.

Oval wire nails are so shaped to prevent wood from splitting. Always drive them in with the wide part along the grain and use them to fix any wood-work that has come adrift.

Picture sprigs are used to hold glass in picture or window frames, or to secure linoleum.

Hardboard pins should always be used to fix hardboard down. The head is shaped so that it sinks into the hardboard and can be covered over.

Chair nails have a decorative round head and are used for all upholstery jobs where the nails are meant to be seen.

Tacks are used for fixing down carpets or fabric.

Floor brads should be used to fix loose floorboards.

Staples secure wire or upholstery webbing on to woodwork. Never use them for electric wire unless they are insulated.

Saddle tacks are a better means of securing electric wire. You drive the tack through the fastener and then clip it over the wire.

Remember, if you are nailing any-thing to anything: always nail the thinner piece of wood to the thicker; do not use more nails than are really needed; and for extra strength drive nails in on opposite slants.

If you have made unsightly dents in the wood after hammering a nail home, you can remove them by cover-ing them with a damp cloth and apply-ing gentle heat with an iron.

Screws

If you need to replace a screw in furniture, or any fixture such as wall brackets or hinges, always use the same type. If the hole is too big for the screw to grip tightly, fit a wall plug or use composition filler, for plaster or masonry. Holes in woodwork can be plugged, if necessary, by jamming them tight with used matches or a Rawlplug. If this does not seem to make the screw secure, try using a slightly longer screw of the same size.

If you find it difficult to loosen a screw, place the screwdriver in one side of the slot at an angle and tap the handle of the screwdriver with a hammer to force the screw in an *anti-clockwise* direction.

Never try to loosen a screw if the head is choked with paint — if the shoulders of the slot become damaged

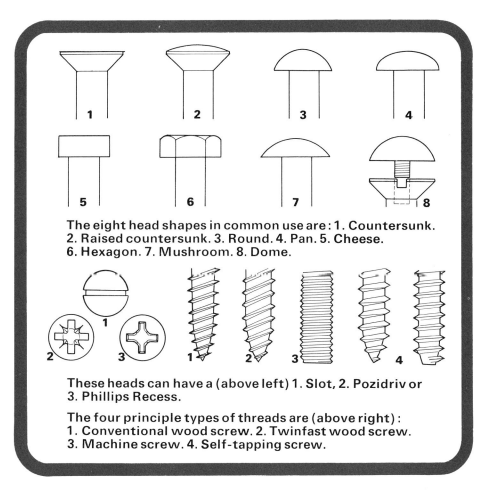

The eight head shapes in common use are: 1. Countersunk. 2. Raised countersunk. 3. Round. 4. Pan. 5. Cheese. 6. Hexagon. 7. Mushroom. 8. Dome.

These heads can have a (above left) 1. Slot, 2. Pozidriv or 3. Phillips Recess.

The four principle types of threads are (above right): 1. Conventional wood screw. 2. Twinfast wood screw. 3. Machine screw. 4. Self-tapping screw.

because the screwdriver will not go in properly, you will never get the screw out. Scratch the paint from around the head of the screw and out of the slot with the point of a bradawl, before you try to turn it.

Countersunk screws have a flat head and are used for most general woodwork. The slope under the head enables the screw to be driven in so that it is flush, or slightly below, the surface of the wood.

Raised Head screws are usually chromium-plated and are used for fixing 'decorative hardware' — door handles, window fasteners, etc.

Dome Head screws are used for fixing mirrors, bath panels and splash-backs. They have a little chromium cap which screws into the head of the screw.

Simple tools for fixing and fastening

Bradawl. Use its sharp point for making holes in wood to make it easier for the screw to be driven in or for starting a hole in plaster walls.

Rawldrill. Will make holes in most solid walls. Must be twisted as it is used to avoid getting it stuck in the masonry.

Hammer. To use with the Rawl-drill or to drive in nails.

Screwdriver. To put screws in or take them out.

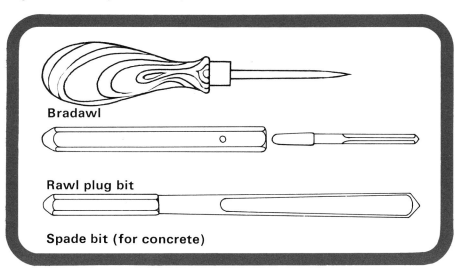

Bradawl

Rawl plug bit

Spade bit (for concrete)

DOORS AND LOCKS

Sticking

Doors which stick: Check the hinges first to make sure that they are not loose. Tighten all the screws on both sides of the hinge and try the door again. If it is no better, slip a piece of carbon paper (chalk might do too, but it's messier) between the door and the frame and keep closing the door on it while you run the paper around the door frame.

Smudges from the carbon will show you exactly where the door is sticking against the frame. Try rubbing these areas with a candle stub to see if it eases the sticking. If it does not, wrap a sheet of medium glasspaper around a small block, then rub down either the door or the frame where the sticking is occuring. Keep trying the door until it opens and closes freely.

Twisted doors

If a door is twisted so badly that one part of it 'closes' before the rest, you may be able to correct it with brute force. Force a thick piece of wood in the frame at the point where the door closes first so that the twist of the door is reversed when it is forced shut. Leave it like that for a few days (if possible), after which the worst of the twist should be corrected.

Rattling doors

If a door rattles it is because the lock is no longer holding it tight against the 'stop' (the frame of wood against which the door closes). One simple solution is to press the door, from outside the room, hard against the lock and measure the gap between the door and the stop. Buy a thin beading of wood thick enough to fill the gap and the same width as the door. Nail this along the face of the

Below left: To stop a door from sticking, slip a piece of carbon paper between the door and frame to ascertain where it is sticking. Make a wedge to jam the door, then plane the edge along the affected area. A good hard rub with rough glasspaper can also remove sufficient thickness to free the door. If the sticking is only very slight, a rub with a candle stub might solve the problem. Below: Reversing a twisted door by force. After a couple of days it should straighten itself.

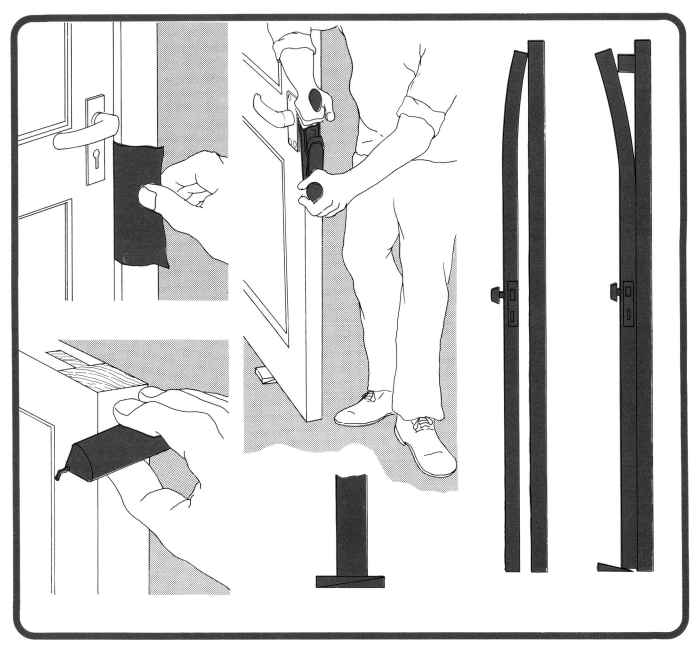

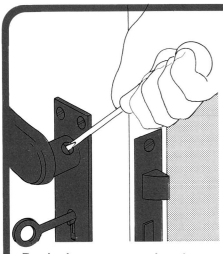

Replacing a conventional mortice lock. Undo one of the handle screws.

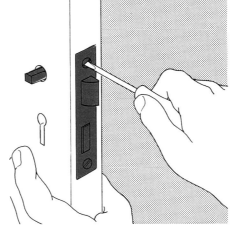

Remove the handles and the handle bar; undo the face plate screws.

Lever the lock from its recess. The new lock will go back in the reverse order.

stop so that the door closes tightly again.

Alternatively, draught-proofing strips may do the trick and eliminate another problem as well. Either fit stick-on, foam plastic strip around the face of the door stop, or nail sprung bronze strip around the frame (see page 26).

Most internal doors now fitted in new houses are made of two sheets of hardboard nailed to a wooden frame. The hardboard sandwiches a fibre 'honeycomb' to give the door rigidity. They are very cheap and perfectly adequate until you want to fix hooks on the back of the door. Screws will go straight through the hardboard and then wave around in the air behind. Either use adhesive hooks, cavity bolts (see page 49), or screw the hook in the centre of the door where there is a strut of the frame.

Creaking hinges
Creaking hinges can easily be cured with a little drop of oil. If you cannot find any, and the noise is driving you mad, use butter or lard. Do not overdo the lubrication of hinges, and always wipe away any surplus oil.

Locks
Most houses have a cylinder lock fitted on the front door, a mortice lock (recessed into the door's edge) on interior doors and either a mortice lock or a rim lock (mounted on the inside face of the door) on the back door.

Cylinder locks need little attention and should be lubricated with powdered graphite (you can buy a graphite puffer to puff it into the lock), rather than oil. If the lock starts to get stiff, an easy way of lubricating the insides is to rub a pencil lead over the key and work it in and out of the slot several times.

Mortice and rim locks which stick

can generally be freed by oiling the latch and keyhole, and, then, vigorously twisting the door knob backwards and forwards. If this does not work, remove the lock from the door, open it up and see if you can find what is wrong. If nothing looks obviously damaged or stuck, take the lock to a shop for repair.

How to remove a mortice lock
1. Undo the screw which holds the inside doorknob; remove it and draw out the handle bar by pulling the outside doorknob.
2. Undo the two screws which are visible in the edge of the door and remove the face plate.
3. Undo the lock-retaining screws under the plate and then lever the lock out of the recess with a screwdriver until you can pull it out by hand.
4. Undo the screws in the side plate

and gently prize it off to expose the works.
5. Check to see that the spring is still intact, that no parts look unusually worn and that nothing is jamming against packed dirt or grease. Clean and oil all the parts.
6. Replace the side plate and try it to see if it works. If it does, replace it in the door following steps 1-4 in the reverse order. If it does not work take it in for repair.

How to remove a rim lock
Rim locks are removed in roughly the same way as are mortice locks except that they are unscrewed from the face of the door rather than the edge. Take off the inside doorknob, remove the handle bar, undo the four screws holding the lock onto the door and then undo the retaining screw at the back of the lock in order to expose the works.

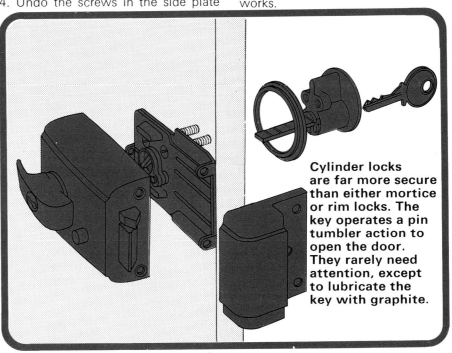

Cylinder locks are far more secure than either mortice or rim locks. The key operates a pin tumbler action to open the door. They rarely need attention, except to lubricate the key with graphite.

WINDOWS

When windows stick

Casement windows (the kind that open outwards on hinges) can be eased by following the same procedures as those recommended for sticking doors (see page 52). Sash windows (the kind that slide up and down) are more difficult to cure if they stick. The most common cause of sticking is a broken sash cord — but replacing it involves removing part of the frame and the window. If both sash cords are intact, try rubbing an ordinary candle stub or bar of soap along the inner frame on each side of the window to lubricate the slides.

Windows in older houses often stick simply because they have been given coat after coat of paint over the years. Removing some of these layers with a proprietary paint stripper, especially from the frame, may be enough to make the window work perfectly again.

Covering a broken window

If a pane of glass is destroyed by some low-flying missile at the weekend it is unlikely — to say the least — that you will have the glass on hand to repair it. A temporary cover made from a piece of polythene sheeting (which will still let the light through) or any kind of waterproof material such as Fablon, will work very satisfactorily for a short time.

Wearing heavy gloves, clear away the broken glass and remove fragments left in the window pane. If there is quite a lot of glass left in the window, always start at the top of the hole and tap it out piece by piece with a small hammer.

Pin the temporary cover to the top of the window frame with drawing

To make temporary repairs to a broken window, cover the entire frame with a sheet of polythene. In order to make it secure it will have to be fixed all around by battens nailed on to the frame. Or two inch carpet tape may be used as shown.

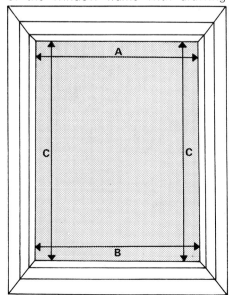

pins or tacks. If you can find any narrow wood battens, nail them around the frame *on top* of the cover. Otherwise, fix the cover all around with drawing pins, and seal any gaps with adhesive tape — waterproof if possible.

Measuring up for new glass

Panes of glass fit into L-shaped rebates on the outside of window frames. Measure the full width and height between the outside edges of this rebate. Be sure that the measurement is the same at both top and bottom of the window, and at both left-hand and right-hand sides. If there is a slight difference, note the *smaller of the two measurements*. Because the glass expands and contracts when it is fitted into a frame, the pane itself must be slightly smaller than the frame to allow for this movement, so deduct 1/8th inch (3 mm) from both the height and the width.

Most glass suppliers will cut a pane to fit if they are given the exact size. Take great care when carrying glass — the best way to hold it is with a thick newspaper wrapped under the bottom edge.

Glass can be very dangerous to handle. Note the correct handling – with gloves.

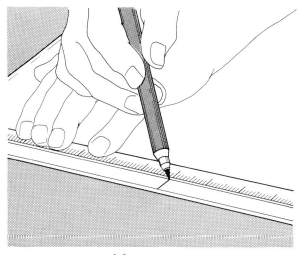

Mark the glass with a wax or Chinagraph pencil.

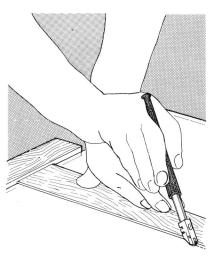

Hold a ruler or straight edge over glass and score along marked lines with an ordinary glass cutter.

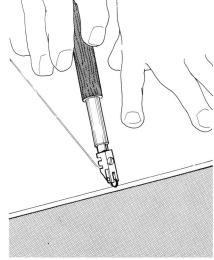

Start scoring at the edge of the glass pane to avoid splintering when it is ready to be broken off.

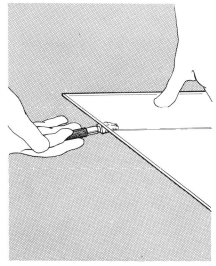

Lift one side of the pane and tap the underside gently with the handle of the glass cutter along the score line.

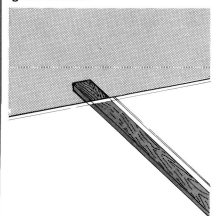

Place pane on the straight edge with score line along one edge. Gloves should be worn for protection.

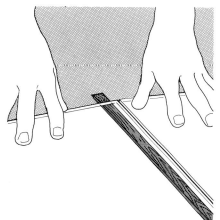

Apply gentle pressure on each side and the pane will snap into two along scored line.

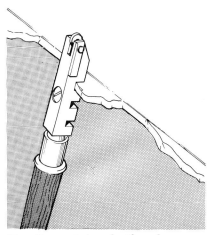

Use the notches in the glass cutter handle to trim edges.

Always wear thick protective gloves when handling broken glass. To remove a broken window pane score around the edge with a glasscutter.

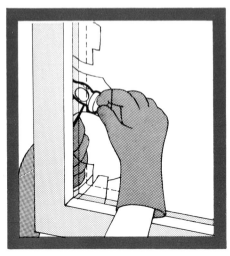

Starting at the top, carefully tap out the glass, piece by piece, with a hammer. Leave the window open if possible.

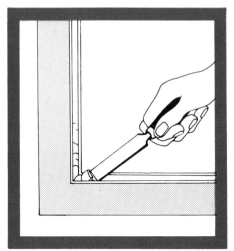

Clear away all the old putty from the rebate around the wooden frame. Some of it may need to be chipped out with a chisel.

Offer up the new pane of glass to make sure it is the right size. Remember it must be slightly undersize to allow for expansion.

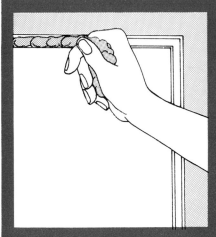

Mould some putty until it is soft and pliable, then press it into the rebate all around the window frame.

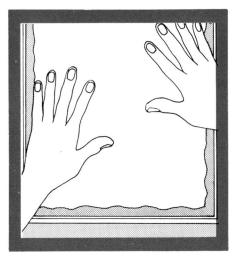

Carefully lift the new pane into position and press it into the putty around the edges only—not in the centre.

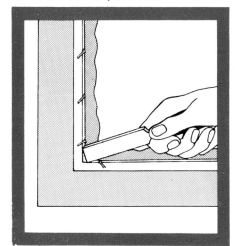

Tap in window sprigs at about 10 inch (254 mm) intervals around the frame to secure the pane of glass in the window.

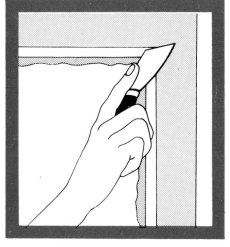

Now press more putty around the glass on the outside of the window and smooth it with a flat-bladed knife.

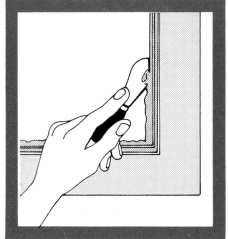

Trim any surplus putty away with a blunt knife —none of it should be visible above the rebate from inside the room.

FURNITURE

Repairing uneven legs

Tables and chairs that wobble because the legs are uneven are maddening. But do not rush to remedy the problem — it is only too easy to get caught in that classic Laurel and Hardy situation of sawing off more and more until the legs just disappear.

First, you should establish whether it is the piece of furniture that is at fault or the floor. A solid, tiled floor should be reasonably flat — try standing the piece of furniture on that. If the same legs wobble wherever you put the piece, they are uneven.

The choice of repair is simple — either add a bit to the leg that is short, or cut a slither off the other three legs. Amputation may seem easiest, but it's not. As only fractions of an inch are normally involved, it is difficult to cut off the legs accurately and squarely; you are quite liable to find a different leg is short when you have finished.

The best way to solve the problem is to use thin scraps of wood to build up the short leg until the chair or table is standing squarely. It is obviously easiest if you can find one piece of the right thickness, but you can glue two or more pieces if really necessary.

Use a metal saw and cut the scraps as close as possible to the shape of the leg (just undersize is better than the other way around). Glue them into position with a PVA adhesive and then, if necessary, fix small panel pins through the pieces to secure them firmly.

A possible alternative solution is to buy nail-on studs (the kind used to prevent scratches on the floor) and to fix one, about the right thickness, to the short leg. Adjust it by hammering it down further into the leg, if necessary.

Wobbly legs

Furniture that takes heavy wear from a growing family sometimes wilts under the strain and, like humans, when furniture weakens it is the legs that show it first.

The legs of tables and chairs can be attached in dozens of different ways, so first of all have a look underneath to see what you can discover.

If you can see any screws (on brackets, blocks or metal plates) tighten them up as hard as you can. If the holes have become too large so that the screws will not fit securely, try removing the old screw and replacing it with a slightly thicker (but not longer) one. If that will not work, fit a rawlplug into the hole; then replace the screw and tighten it up.

This simple repair may solve the entire problem, but if not (or if you cannot see any screws to tighten), turn the piece of furniture upside down on an old sheet of newspaper and find out exactly which bits are loose. Use one foot to hold a table steady, and try to wobble each table leg. Put chairs upside down with the seat on a table so that you can hold the seat steady and try the legs.

When you know which parts are loose, buy a metal bracket of a suitable shape to hold the pieces together underneath the table or chair, where it will not be noticed. If you are not quite sure what shape you will need, take a look at the brackets shown here and see if any of them will serve the purpose. If not, make a little drawing and take it to an ironmonger to explain the problem.

Be very sure that you buy the right size screws to fit whatever bracket you use. To fix it, hold it in place and mark the position for the screws with a pencil. Use a bradawl to make holes to start the screws off. Fix one side of the bracket first, then the other. Insert the screws into the holes and, using a screwdriver, drive them in as tight as they will go.

Cabinet doors

Most problems with doors on furniture can be cured by making adjustments to the hinges.

If a door keeps *springing open*, the hinges are set in too deep. Cut a piece of thin cardboard (about the thickness of a cereal packet) exactly the same size as one leaf of the hinge. Dealing with one hinge at a time, take out the screws on the cabinet side, slip the cardboard into the recess behind the hinge, then replace the screws. If this has not cured the problem completely, pack out the hinges on the door side in the same way.

If a door has *dropped*, pack out the cabinet side of the bottom hinge

Useful brackets for securing wobbly legs or wonky furniture

Choose a shape that will be unobtrusive as well as practical.

Make sure the screws are driven home tightly or the bracket will not work.

Where appearance does not matter, a wooden support nailed in place works as well.

Packing out hinges with thin pieces of cardboard can cure problem doors.

only. If the door has three hinges, put two thicknesses of cardboard behind the bottom hinge and one behind the centre hinge.

If the top of a door *binds*, the top hinge is set too deeply. Pack out the cabinet side of the top hinge only.

If the hinges *jam* it is probably because the screw heads are projecting above the surface of the hinge. Drive them in until they are flush with the hinge; if they are too big, replace them with smaller gauge screws and fill out the holes with rawlplugs

Drawers
Drawers either slide on side runners or on the bottom edges of their sides. It is easy to tell which is which: drawers with a groove in the sides slide on side runners, drawers with plain sides slide on their bottoms.

If you are moving to a newly built house, you may find the drawers in your furniture will begin to stick — do not do anything about them for at least a month to give the timber a chance to shrink and adjust to the moisture content of the house.

A drawer that is completely jammed can be released by switching on a fan heater about three or four feet away and leaving it directed at the piece of furniture for an hour or so. Do *not* do this to an antique piece.

To ease a drawer that sticks, take it out and rub down the runners with medium grade glasspaper until they are perfectly smooth. Then, do the same for the runners in the cabinet, so that where the drawer comes into contact with the cabinet both sides are clean and smooth. Wipe away any dust and then rub a bar of soap or a candle stub hard all over the areas you have smoothed down.

Handles
Most modern furniture handles are held in place by washers and screws which only need tightening when the handle becomes loose. The handles on older furniture, however, were simply glued in place, with the result that they frequently come away in your hand—particularly if you are in a hurry and have tried to wrench a door or drawer open.

To replace such a handle, carefully scrape away all remnants of the old glue, then coat both hole and handle with PVA adhesive and press the handle back into place.

If, as sometimes inexplicably happens, the hole seems too large for the handle, cut a small piece of felt, or a similar thick fabric, and stick that around the handle before you put it into the hole.

If modern screw-on handles pull out of their fixing, plug the hole with a rawlplug to ensure that the handle stays fixed when you screw it back.

Castors
Castors are normally held in little metal or plastic sleeves set into the leg of a chair, bed, or other piece of furniture. If a castor drops off from a heavy piece of furniture which is rarely lifted from the floor, do not bother completely replacing it. Simply pop it back into its little hole and hold it there until the piece of furniture is lowered on to it.

If, however, it is something that you are constantly lifting, it is irritating to leave the castor wheels behind every time you pick it up. To replace castors, turn the piece of furniture upside down and prise the metal or plastic sleeve out of the leg with a screwdriver.

Take it with you when you buy a replacement so that you are certain to buy one that fits the existing hole in the leg.

To fit a replacement castor, just press the sleeve into the hole and gently tap it down with a hammer until the little spikes in the collar bite deeply into the wood.

Mending a small upholstery tear
Snip off any loose threads around the tear, but do not cut away the actual material. Cut a new piece of fabric (any kind) slightly longer than the actual tear and ease it underneath, making sure it is quite flat. Gently pull back the edges of the tear and smear a PVA adhesive on both the patch and the under edges of the tear with an old knife. Wait until it is tacky, press down one edge at a time and then press the edges together.

Replacing a button
You will need a 10-inch mattress needle and mattress twine. Thread the needle so that one end of the twine is only a few inches long. Insert the needle in the spot where the button is missing and push it through the chair until the point emerges on the other side. Gently pull the needle until the eye disappears and then push the eye back through, close to the insertion point, so that the twine is threaded behind the cover of the chair. Unthread and remove the needle. Thread the button onto one of the ends of the twine and secure it with a tight slip knot. Push the button into its recess

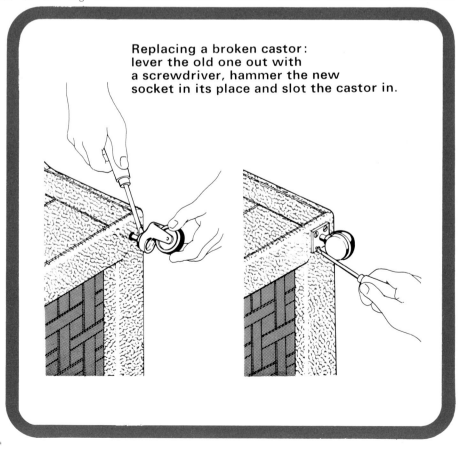

Replacing a broken castor: lever the old one out with a screwdriver, hammer the new socket in its place and slot the castor in.

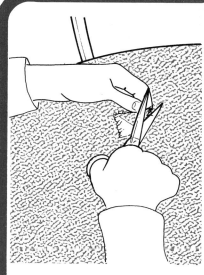

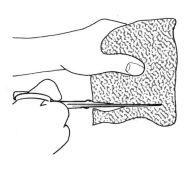

To mend an upholstery tear, first snip away any loose threads, but do not cut away the actual material.

Cut a new piece of tough fabric slightly wider and longer than the tear—it need not necessarily match.

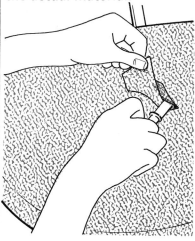

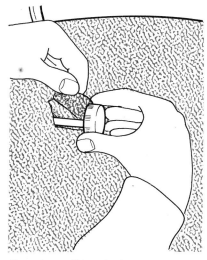

Ease it underneath the tear, so that it is flat and roughly in the centre.

Gently pull back the edges of the tear and smear a PVA adhesive on the back of the upholstery fabric . . .

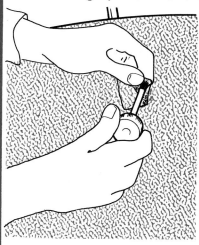

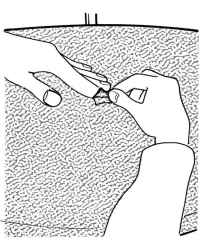

. . . and on as much of the patch as is accessible. Use an old knife to spread the adhesive under the fabric.

Wait until the adhesive is tacky, then press down one edge at a time and gently push them together.

in the chair fabric and tie one or two more tight knots. Trim off the ends of the thread.

Deckchairs
Never wait until you have fallen through a deckchair to replace the canvas; as soon as it shows signs of wear, take it off and replace it.

It is usually possible to buy ready-cut lengths of canvas for deckchairs, complete with large-headed nails for fixing. Canvas composed of man-made fibres lasts longer than natural canvas, but you may not think it looks as attractive.

To re-cover a deckchair, shut it flat and lay the canvas between the top and bottom rails. It should be taut, but not stretched. Fold back a flap about $\frac{3}{4}$in. (19mm) deep; wrap it around the rails and nail through the two thicknesses of canvas on the underside of the rail (the inside edges when the deckchair is flat) at each end.

Repairing furniture finishes
All repairs to furniture should only be used for very minor or superficial blemishes. *Never* treat a piece of furniture yourself if you suspect it to be of any value. Have it appraised by an expert before attempting to work on it.

Blisters in veneer should be cut along the wood grain with a sharp knife or single-edged razor blade. Using the blade of the knife, ease an animal glue into the cut, then cover the blister with a piece of aluminium foil and apply gentle warmth with an iron. After a minute or so, turn the iron off but leave its weight on the area until the glue has set.

Peeled veneer is best re-stuck with a PVA adhesive. Raise the loose area with the thin blade of a knife, but be careful not to bend it back too far or the veneer will crack. Gently scrape away the old glue with another knife, then apply a PVA adhesive to both surfaces. Pile some heavy weights (books will do) on to the surface and allow it to set overnight.

Scratches can be rubbed out with paper dipped in linseed oil or with a proprietary scratch remover. Melted beeswax stained darker than the wood can be used to fill deep scratches or cigarette burns. Rub it well into the wood once it is nearly set and polish over it.

Shallow cigarette burns can be rubbed out with glasspaper and coloured in with matching artists' oil paint. Repolish when dry.

White patches on cellulose or lacquer finishes, or on French-polished surfaces, are usually due to excessive heat. Remove them with a proprietary ring remover or use a 1:1 solution of *real* turpentine and linseed oil. Clean this off with vinegar and repeat the process until the mark has gone.

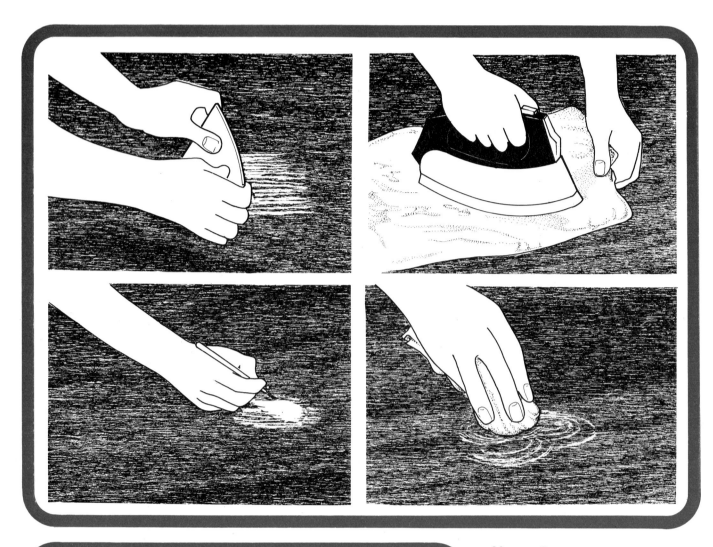

Above: One method of removing bruises from polished surfaces involves the use of a damp cloth and an iron. Firstly, remove the surrounding polish with the aid of a cabinet scraper. Place a piece of damp cloth over the bruise and press with a hot iron. The steam will cause the timber to swell back into its original shape. Using oil paints, blend the damaged area in with the surrounding wood and polish thoroughly.

Left: Replacing the canvas on a deckchair. Using a mallet and old screwdriver remove the tacks. Fold back a flap about 3″ (19 mm) at each end and tack it to the underside of the top and bottom rails – the inside edges when the deckchair is flat. The canvas should be taut but not stretched.

Water which has seeped beneath the surface of polish often causes *black marks*. Repair these by removing the surface (with glasspaper) and then applying a saturated solution of oxalic acid crystals and water (a mixture in which no more crystals will dissolve). This solution may also be applied to superficial *ink stains*, but beware as it is highly poisonous.

Polished surfaces which have *badly damaged areas* should be carefully rubbed down to the bare wood with fine glasspaper — take care not to form sharp edges with the surrounding polish. Stain the wood with a naptha stain (Colron is a good one), then build up the surface with several coats of proprietary French polish in the appropriate colour.

When it is dry, rub down the entire surface with a fine pumice powder, wipe away all traces of the powder and polish with a good wax polish.

Superficial *alcohol marks* on a semi-matt finish can sometimes be removed with fine steel wool.

Cellulose or lacquered finishes should be repaired with a polyurethane lacquer. Rub down the damaged area with fine glasspaper then build up the surface with successive thin coats of polyurethane. Leave it overnight to harden, then rub the finish level with a fine abrasive paper. For a matt finish, rub over the entire surface with finest steel wool, 00 or 000 gauge. Finish with wax polish.

Oiled finishes (normally teak or afrormosia) which have become dirty and sticky because too much oil has been applied, can be cleaned by rubbing them thoroughly with a cloth soaked in *real* turpentine. Use plenty of cloth to wipe off the dissolved oil, then give the surface a thin rub over with linseed oil or teak oil.

Bruises on wooden furniture should be treated as soon as possible. Scrape all traces of polish from the affected area then make a firm pad of cotton wool wrapped with a clean, soft cloth. Soak the pad in boiling water and apply it to the bruise, wiping off any water that seeps on to surrounding surfaces. Keep the water on the boil and give repeated applications until the bruises have disappeared. Leave it for several hours to dry, then sand the affected area with a fine abrasive paper, stain it, if necessary, to match, and polish.

Small patches on *painted furniture* can be matched by using a white undercoat which has been tinted with artists' oil paint. It will dry out a tone darker so use a colour slightly lighter than the original.

To match gloss, use a paint undercoat and finish with *clear* varnish. Revarnish the entire surface to get an even texture. To reproduce an antique finish, rub a bit of soot into the wet paint along edges and in corners.

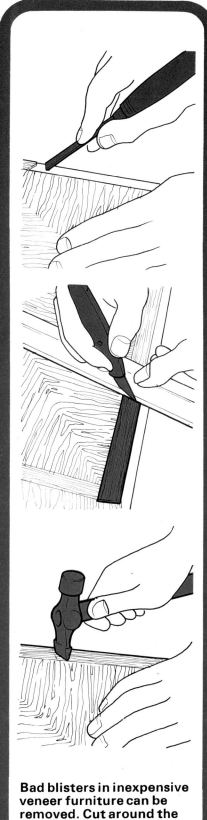

Bad blisters in inexpensive veneer furniture can be removed. Cut around the blister and scrape away the glue underneath. Then match in a new piece of veneer and cut in with a sharp knife. Dampen the veneer, apply a PVA adhesive and, using a Warrington hammer, squeeze out excess glue.

HOW TO CARE... SO YOU NEED NOT REPAIR

Knowing what to repair, when and how may save the day; but knowing how to take care of things so that they will need few repairs saves time and worry, too.

Modern living can sometimes seem to be a maze of things — useful, helpful things perhaps, but still things which can seem unfamiliar and puzzling without advice on how to treat them. What, for example, can you do for a kettle that has become clogged with mineral deposits from the water supply? Or, how can you eliminate the cat's fur from your special chair — without eliminating the cat? Hints and advice on problems such as these follow.

Kitchens

Bottles. To remove smells from bottles try half filling the bottle with cold water to which you have added a spoonful of dry mustard. Shake it up and let it stand for 15 to 20 minutes. Rinse well. If this does not work, try a mixture of warm water, a spoonful of tea leaves and a spoonful of vinegar. Allow this to stand for several hours, and then rinse well.

Brushes. Bristles in brushes can be straightened by holding them over steam for a minute or two and rubbing gently.

China and crockery. It is best never to wash crockery in boiling water or to use a powder detergent—these tend to ruin the pattern. Most discolorations can be removed by rubbing with a solution of vinegar and salt. Tea stains can be removed by soaking the dish overnight in hot soda water and then rubbing with a cloth dipped in the vinegar-salt solution.

If you should get a simple breakage in a dish, try mending it with an epoxy-based resin, such as Araldite.

Corks. If a cork sticks, try rubbing it with a bit of Vaseline. Corks that are soaked first in warm water are easier to cut.

Cutlery. All cutlery can easily be stained by everyday items such as salt, egg, vinegar, and even water. Some stains are faster-acting than others, so do wash any cutlery as soon as possible — and to make it really sparkle, hand dry and buff it.

Silver or silver plate cutlery should be kept in a place with a soft lining so that it will not get scratched; any silver not in use should be kept in an airtight container to prevent tarnishing. Polish silver regularly with a special polish (which, incidentally, should *never* be used on stainless steel).

One further caution, cutlery with handles made of natural materials such as wood, bone, and even some plastics should not be soaked in water or put in a dishwasher as their adhesive fixing may become soft and the handle will then drop off. Should this happen, scrape out the loose cement from the slit in the handle and fill it with a powdered resin adhesive and a drop of ordinary candle wax. Hold the knife with a piece of cloth or a protective glove and heat the spike end of the knife. Press it into the handle, rinse in warm water and wipe away any excess adhesive.

Drains. To keep drains fresh, rinse regularly with hot, strong soda water — this is especially effective for cutting accumulations of grease. Disinfectants can be used to combat smells.

Glassware. Never subject glass to extremes of temperature — it's one of the surest ways to break it. If you put a glass under a hot tap, always heat the outside first to allow for expansion and prevent cracking.

Should two tumblers stick together, fill the inner one with cool water and set the outer one in warm water; one will contract and the other expand so they will be easy to separate.

Glass stained by wine, hard water or similar substances can be cleaned by rinsing with cool water and vinegar. Glasses which have contained milk should be rinsed with cold water before washing. Wash glasses in warm, never very hot, water with a mild liquid detergent.

Cut glass can be cleaned with an old toothbrush and dried with jeweller's sawdust.

Porcelain. Stains can often be removed from porcelain with a bit of lemon juice or vinegar. Small cracks can sometimes be sealed with an epoxy-based resin, such as Araldite.

Pots and pans. The care of pots and pans depends upon the material of which they are made. *Aluminium* pans are light and very easy to clean. Use a liquid detergent and nylon or fine steel wool scouring pads, never copper ones. *Never* use washing soda as it has an adverse chemical reaction on aluminium. If possible do not keep food or liquids in aluminium as it may cause unsightly pit marks. Metal spoons can scratch, so beware of using them.

Cast iron pans are extremely durable, but rather on the heavy side. They are almost always protected against rust with an enamel covering of some sort. If not they should be treated before using by heating a bit

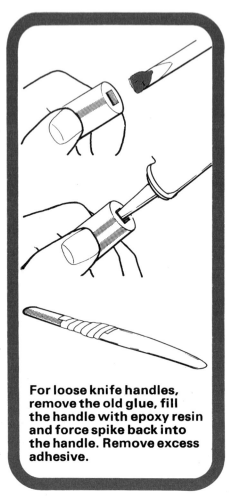

For loose knife handles, remove the old glue, fill the handle with epoxy resin and force spike back into the handle. Remove excess adhesive.

of oil (olive or cooking) in them, allowing it to cool, and then wiping off with greaseproof paper. Cast iron can be washed in hot soapy water, but it should always be thoroughly dried to prevent rusting.

Copperware can be cleaned of tarnishes by rubbing hard with a piece of lemon which has been dipped in a bit of salt and vinegar.

Enamelled cooking ware is liable to scratch so abrasives should not be used on it. Soaking in warm water and liquid detergent will usually remove most baked-on substances.

Non-stick coatings on pans must never be scratched or scraped. Use medium heat settings for cooking, and clean in warm, soapy water.

Steel frying pans can be treated against rust as are cast-iron ones.

Tinware that has become very dirty should be washed in a solution of water and bicarbonate of soda and then rinsed well. Dry thoroughly to prevent rust.

As a general rule, never take dishes or pans straight from the oven or stove and plunge them into the sink for washing — they could easily warp.

Refrigerator. To remove smells from a refrigerator, keep a dish of powdered charcoal inside, or a few drops of oil of wintergreen.

Scumming is a result of hard water deposits on metal surfaces. Special capsules are often available which can be put in hard water to soften it.

Steam irons and kettles especially must be protected against scumming.

Steamed windows. To prevent windows from steaming up rub them with a cloth which has been soaked in equal quantities of glycerine and methylated spirits.

Laundry
Bleaching. Yellowed clothing that is washable can be restored by adding 1 teaspoon of powdered borax to the last rinse.

Colour. Colour can often be restored to clothes by sponging them with vinegar and water. To prevent colours from running, wash them in tepid water and use a detergent with some salt (never use soap and salt).

Bedroom
Blankets. Care of blankets depends upon the material of which they are made. If they are specially treated for moths at the manufacturing stage, then you need worry no further — look at the label to see. Most wool blankets need dry cleaning.

To restore fluffiness in some blankets, try rubbing them in sections with a fine wire brush.

Mattresses. Be sure to remove any polythene coverings from mattresses before using them — if not, condensation and mildew may occur. Do not wash mattress ticking, rather try cleaning spots with dry cleaning fluid.

Sheets. Always wash deeply dyed sheets and pillowcases separately the first few times, as they may run slightly. They should not fade, however.

Quilts. The new continental quilts replace blankets and top sheets. They should be given an occasional airing outdoors. Cleaning depends upon the fillings: synthetic fillings can be hand or machine washed, or dry cleaned if you prefer; down and feather quilts should be dry cleaned. Air out any coverings that have been dry cleaned before using.

Sitting rooms
Upholstery. Upholstered furniture is best cleaned with a relatively stiff brush, or a soft one for delicate fabrics. Dry cleaning fluid may be applied with a pad and rubbed in gently with a circular movement over the entire piece.

Animal fur is often difficult to remove from some types of upholstery. If brushing or using a vacuum cleaner is unsuccessful, try wiping with a damp cloth (be sure it's not wet). Failing that, try sticky tape; it may be slow, but it usually works.

Lampshades. Paper, cotton and fabric shades are generally the most delicate. Dust them very lightly and if possible only hold them by the wire fittings. Dirty marks can be removed sometimes with a *slightly* damp cloth. Do not wet these types of shades.

STAIN REMOVAL GUIDE

To be effective, stain removal requires an abundance of knowledge about the nature of the stain and the nature of the material from which it is to be removed. When in doubt, consult someone who knows or you may find yourself with a complete mess instead of a small mark.

Most stains can be removed almost completely if prompt action is taken, so do not wait for days before tackling such a problem. Whatever you use as a removal agent, find out beforehand what it will do to a material — sometimes a stain is better than a hole. And *beware* of the possible dangers from proprietary cleaning agents — some are flammable, some give off poisonous vapours, and others are deadly poisonous if tasted, by a child, for instance.

Fabrics

Washable fabrics. Stains caused by . . .

Alcohol. Blot immediately, rinse in cold water, then launder.

Cocoa, Coffee, Tea, Milk, Fruit, Soft Drinks, Some Wines. Blot, then launder in a solution of 1 oz. borax to 1 pint warm water.

Blood, Egg. Rinse immediately in cold water.

Burns, Scorches. Soak in glycerine or sponge with a solution of 1 oz. borax to 1 pint water.

Fat. Rub gently with carbon tetrachloride or a proprietary stain remover.

Glue. Soak in water as hot as possible without damaging the fabric. If stain persists, soak in warmed white vinegar for one minute, then launder.

Ink. Sponge with detergent suds. Sprinkle white fabrics with a solution of lemon juice and salt; leave for an hour and launder.

Ballpoint Pens. Hold a cloth dampened with methylated spirits against the stain. Launder.

Mildew. Apply lemon juice and leave to dry.

Oil, Grease, Tar. Sponge with turpentine, rinse and launder.

Paint. Dab turpentine on oil-based paint. Soak emulsion paint stains in cold water.

Saline Liquids, Urine. Rinse in clean water. Then immerse in a solution consisting of an egg cup of white vinegar to 1 pint water. Rinse and launder.

Fabrics that should be dry-cleaned. Stains caused by . . . .

Alcohol. Blot immediately and sponge with a solution of 1 teaspoon white vinegar to 1 pint water.

Cocoa, Coffee, Tea, Milk, Soft Drinks. Blot, then apply carbon tetrachloride or a proprietary stain remover.

Blood, Egg. Dab with a solution of 2 drops of ammonia to a cupful of cold water. If stain persists, make a paste of cold water and washing starch, let it dry on the stain then brush it off.

Burns, Scorches. Make a paste of borax and glycerine. Let it dry on the stain, then brush it off and sponge with a damp cloth.

Fat. Rub gently with carbon tetrachloride or a proprietary stain remover.

Fruit. Wipe with methylated spirits or pure alcohol. Apply a proprietary stain remover.

Glue. Sponge with detergent suds, then rub liquid detergent into the stain. Sponge with cold water.

Ink. Sponge with detergent suds. Sprinkle white fabrics with a solution of lemon juice and salt.

Ballpoint Pens. Dab with a cloth dampened with methylated spirits.

Mildew. Moisten with lemon juice, sprinkle with salt and leave to dry, outside if possible. Then sponge gently.

Oil, Grease, Tar. Sponge with a little turpentine, then with clean water.

Paint. Dab turpentine on oil-based paints, then sponge with clean water. Sponge emulsion paint stains with cold water.

Saline Liquids, Urine — Sponge with a solution of 1 egg-cup of white vinegar to 1 pint water.

All other stains should be treated with a solution of detergent in hot water. Always work *inwards* from the edge of the stain.

Carpets

Stains caused by Cocoa, Coffee, Ink, Milk, Soft Drinks, Tea, Fruit Juices, Grass, Paint, Rust, Salt Liquids, Mineral Water, Medicinal Salts, Soot, Starchy Food and Shoe Polish should be treated as follows:

1. Mop up or scrape away as much of the spilled material as possible.
2. Apply carbon tetrachloride or trichlorethylene with an old towel. Starting on the outside edge and working towards the centre, rub with a circular movement. Keep re-folding the cloth and moistening it with the cleaning solution, and continue wiping and blotting the carpet. Be sure to work in a well-ventilated room.

If fruit stains persist, rub them with methylated spirits.

Rub grass stains with methylated spirits before applying the cleaning fluid.

If rust stains persist, rub the area with a warm solution of oxalic acid (obtainable from a chemist), then rinse the stain with water and blot.

Stains from urine or saline liquids which persist, should be rubbed with a mild detergent solution mixed with vinegar (one egg-cupful of vinegar to one pint of detergent solution).

Stains caused by Beer, Spirits, Oil and Grease, Tar, Wax, Wines and Ballpoint pens . . . .

1. Mop up or scrape away as much of the spilled material as possible. (For spilled wax, hold an iron over the spot to loosen the carpet fibre.)
2. Mix a proprietary carpet shampoo with lukewarm water until it lathers. Apply the solution to the stain with an old towel, wiping and blotting the carpet frequently, and adding more lather until the stain disappears. Repeat the wiping and blotting with clean water to remove the lather. Do not soak the carpet.

Stains caused by oil, grease or tar may need a separate treatment with carbon tetrachloride or trichlorethylene after the carpet shampoo solution has been applied.

Stains caused by the ink from ballpoint pens should be wiped with a mixture of methylated spirits and white vinegar. Apply the solution with an old towel and blot frequently to prevent the stain from spreading.

Spilled salt should be vacuumed up as soon as possible — it attracts moisture and will discolour a carpet.

Water spilled in large quantities on a carpet should be mopped up and blotted with a clean, dry towel. If possible lift the carpet to assist in drying. To prevent permanent staining sponge the area with a solution of one egg-cupful of vinegar in a gallon of cold water.

All other carpet stains should be treated with a solution of detergent in hot water. Always work inwards from the edge of the stain.

Many cleaning fluids are poisonous — keep them away from children. If doubtful about colour-fastness, always test a small unnoticeable area first.

Wallpaper

With *colourfast* wallpapers use a mild detergent in water to remove stains. Work from the bottom upwards to keep the paper from getting too wet. Proprietary cleaning fluids will remove *grease spots*.

Use aerosol 'dry' cleaners on *non-washable* papers. Spray the stain with the cleaning material, leave it to dry then lightly brush away the white powder residue.

Dry cleaning fluid will help remove stains caused by adhesive tape, candle wax, chewing gum, crayons, cosmetics, creosote, felt-tip pens, gravy, grease, ice cream, marking ink, milk, mineral waters, mustard, oils, plasticine, polish, sealing wax, soot, tar and typewriter ribbons.

Amyl acetate will help remove stains caused by nail varnish, perfume polyurethane or cellulose lacquer.

Methylated spirits or surgical spirits will help remove stains caused by adhesive tape, ballpoint ink, carbon paper, felt-tip pens, grass, hair lacquer, indelible pencil, mustard, nail varnish, sealing wax, shellac varnish, spinach, wax polish.

Glycerine will help remove stains caused by bottled sauces, creosote, fruit juice, grass, spinach, tar, wine.

Mineral turpentine substitute will help remove stains caused by creosote, indian ink, polyurethane lacquer, tar, typewriter ribbons, wax polish.

One tablespoonful of cloudy ammonia in $\frac{1}{2}$ pint of water will help remove stains caused by battery acid, marking ink, perspiration.

Equal parts of peroxide and water will help remove stains caused by bottled sauces, beer, coffee, fruit juices, ice lollies, iodine, jam, mildew, mineral waters, nicotine, scorch marks, spirits, tea, wine.

Enzyme detergent suds will help remove stains caused by bird droppings, blood, chocolate, cocoa, egg, jelly, mineral waters, spirits, starch, urine.

Floors

On wooden floors, remove stains by rubbing them carefully with wire wool soaked in mineral turpentine substitute.

On unsealed cork, use fine glass-paper or wire wool to rub out marks, but take great care not to damage the cork tiles.

On linoleum, remove stains with wire wool and liquid paraffin.

On plastic tiles, use liquid wax remover, *never* turpentine, mineral turpentine substitutes or paraffin.

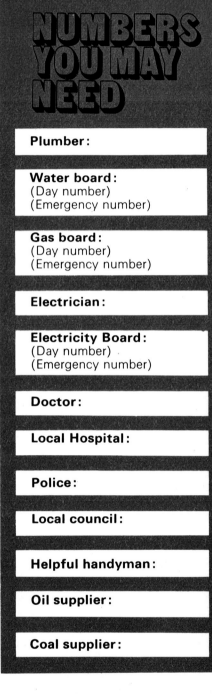

NUMBERS YOU MAY NEED

Plumber:

Water board:
(Day number)
(Emergency number)

Gas board:
(Day number)
(Emergency number)

Electrician:

Electricity Board:
(Day number)
(Emergency number)

Doctor:

Local Hospital:

Police:

Local council:

Helpful handyman:

Oil supplier:

Coal supplier:

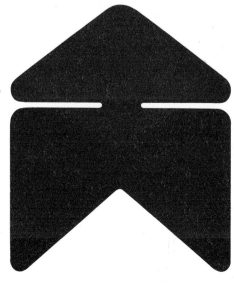

DATA SHEETS

A guide to household tools and equipment
If you've ever rummaged through a pile of miscellaneous tools without knowing which one to select for a specific job, then the following DATA SHEETS will be a valuable guide. All the common household tools that you'll be using for household repairs are illustrated in full colour with a detailed breakdown of their various uses.

By using this DATA SHEET section as a reference guide, you'll choose the right tool for the job which can save time, temper – and money. Included tools are:

Hammers	Screwdrivers	Saws
Cramping and Clamping Tools		Spanners
Wrenches	Pliers	Bradawls
Measuring and Marking Tools		Pincers
Bricklaying Tools	Equipment for Upholstery	

There is also a helpful DATA SHEET on how to treat soils or stains in fabrics which will not come out with normal laundering. The final DATA SHEET tells you what kind of adhesives are available on the market, how to treat material before glueing, and what types of glue will stick different materials together.

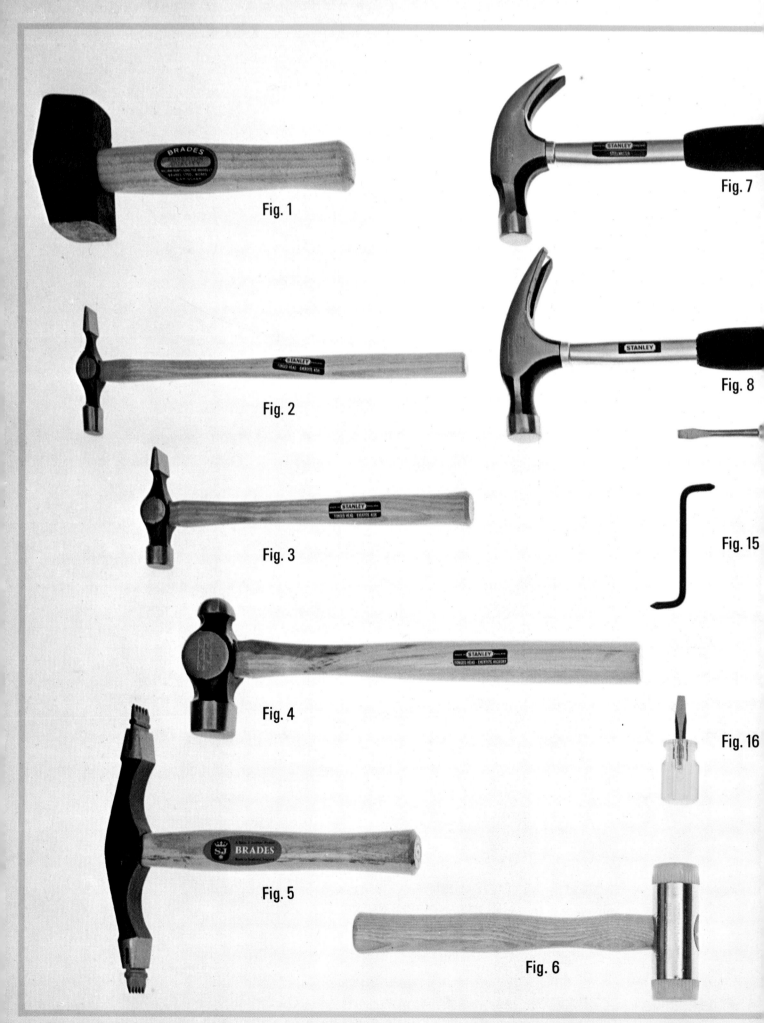

Fig. 1

Fig. 2

Fig. 3

Fig. 4

Fig. 5

Fig. 6

Fig. 7

Fig. 8

Fig. 15

Fig. 16

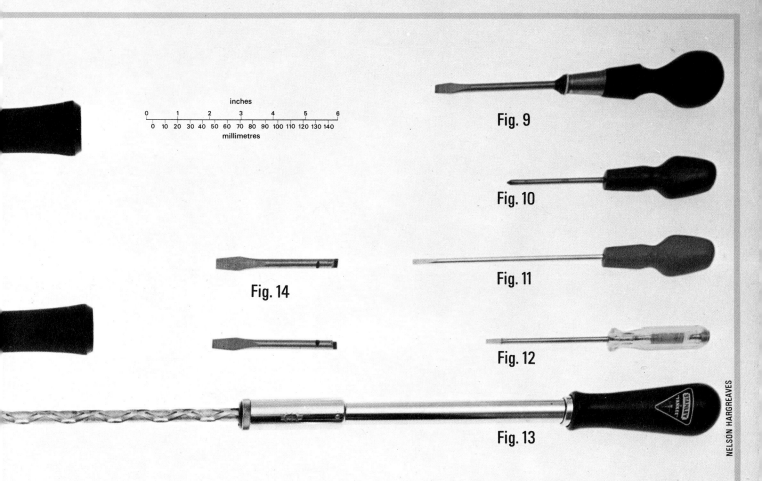

inches
0 1 2 3 4 5 6

0 10 20 30 40 50 60 70 80 90 100 110 120 130 140
millimetres

Fig. 9

Fig. 10

Fig. 14

Fig. 11

Fig. 12

Fig. 13

NELSON HARGREAVES

DATA SHEET

Hammers and Screwdrivers

The right tool for the job makes all the difference—saving time, tempers and often money as well. The range of choice for even simple tools such as hammers and screwdrivers is extremely wide, and each one is designed with a particular task in mind. This DATA SHEET will help you match tool to task.

Hammers range in function from those used for heavy demolition work to those appropriate to fine nailing. In addition, each type of hammer comes in various weights.

Fig.1. Club hammer. 2½-4lb (1130-1800g). Used for general heavy hammering, particularly in building and demolition work. In conjunction with a bolster chisel it is used for cutting bricks, shaping paving stones, knocking through brickwork and so on. The *sledge hammer* (not shown) has a straight sided head, a 3ft handle, weighs between 4 and 14lb (1.8-6.4Kg) and is used for driving metal stakes, demolition work and so on.

Fig.2. Pin or telephone hammer. 3½-4oz (100-110g). Used for tacks, panel pins, fine nailing and bradding. The wedge shaped end is

used for starting small nails while holding them between your fingers.

Fig.3. Warrington or cross pein hammer. 6-16oz (170-450g). Used for general nailing, joinery, and planishing or metal beating.

Fig.4. Ball pein or engineer's hammer. 4oz-31lb (110-1360g). Used for metal working. The round end is used for starting rivets, for example. This is the hammer to use for *masonry nails* as its hardened steel face will not chip.

Fig.5. Scutch or comb hammer. Used for trimming and shaping common or hard bricks which would damage a brick trowel. The combs can be replaced after wear.

Fig.6. Soft-headed hammer. Used in metal beating and in general work where it is important not to damage a surface. The soft head also avoids the possibility of a spark setting of an explosion. Replaceable heads may be made of plastic, lead, copper or leather.

Fig.7. Claw hammer. 16-24oz (450-570g). Used for general purpose carpentry, particularly for driving and removing nails. When taking out nails, make sure the nail head is well into the claw and lever evenly.

Fig.8. Ripping claw hammer. Used similarly to the claw hammer in work where speed rather than care is essential.

Screwdrivers, too, have a range of functions and sizes. Match the screwdriver tip as closely as possible to the screw slot to prevent damage to either.

Fig.9. Standard slotted screwdriver. Used for general screwdriving of single slotted screws.

Fig.10. Crosshead screwdriver (Pozidriv or Philips). Used with cross slotted screws to provide greater purchase and positive location.

Fig.11. Parallel tip screwdriver. Used in engineering, and otherwise, when the screw sits inside a recess of the same width.

Fig.12. Electrical screwdriver. The insulated handle contains a neon indicator which lights when the blade is touched against a live source. You must ensure that the insulation is safe for the voltages you intend to check.

Fig.13. Archimedean (or Yankee) spiral ratchet screwdriver. Used for general purpose screwdriving. Pushing the handle home automatically drives or removes screws. When locked, at length or closed, the ratchet allows screws to be driven or removed without taking the blade from the slot. **Fig.14.** The chuck can take blades of different widths, and even drill bits.

Fig.15. Double-ended cranked screwdriver. Used for driving awkwardly-placed screws.

Fig.16. Stub screwdriver. Used in confined spaces. You can grip the square shank with a spanner to give greater purchase.

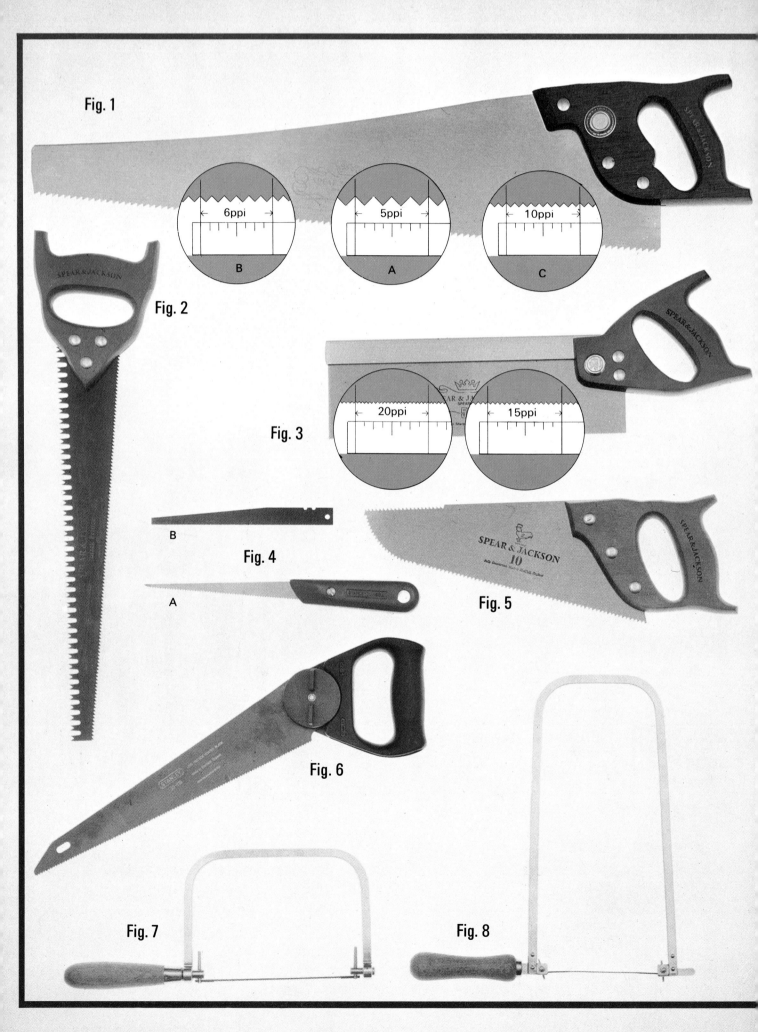

Fig. 1

Fig. 2

B
6ppi

A
5ppi

C
10ppi

Fig. 3

20ppi

15ppi

B

Fig. 4

A

SPEAR & JACKSON
10

Fig. 5

Fig. 6

Fig. 7

Fig. 8

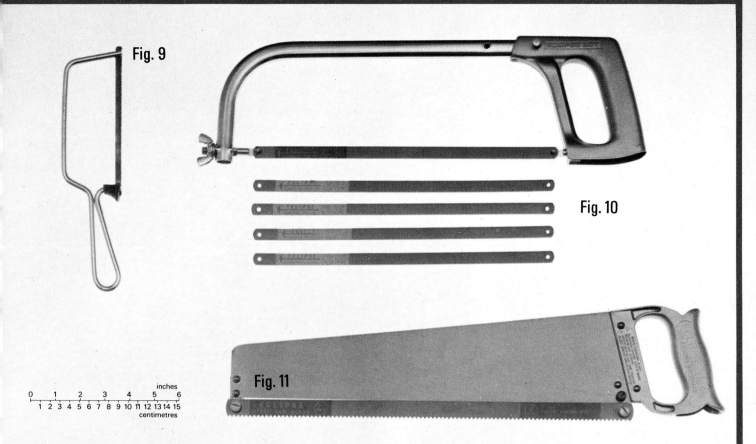

Fig. 9

Fig. 10

Fig. 11

```
        0     1     2     3     4     5     6   inches
        1 2 3 4 5 6 7 8 9 10 11 12 13 14 15
                              centimetres
```

DATA SHEET
Saws

Efficient and easy cutting is a prime requirement of all do-it-yourself jobs. There are a wide range of saws available to enable you to do just this—and this DATA SHEET tells you all about them.

The type of saw you use for a job depends on the material you are using, how accurate the cutting needs to be and where the job is located. Knowing which saw to use will simplify all do-it-yourself jobs.

Knowledge of a few technical terms will help explain the DATA SHEET:

Points per inch (ppi) refers to the number of saw teeth to the inch along the saw blade. Woodworking saws with a small number of ppi are suitable for cutting softwoods and those with a larger number should be used for sawing hardwoods.

The *kerf* is the name given to the width of the saw cut.

The *gullet* is the distance between one saw tooth and the next. The gullet carries sawdust out of the kerf to make the task of sawing easier. Saws suitable for cutting softwoods have larger gullets than those suitable for hardwoods—this is because softwoods tend to produce more waste material than hardwoods.

Fig.1. Hand saw. There are 3 types of hand saw: **A.** Rip saw. 26in. (661mm) long with 5 ppi. It is used for cutting softwoods working *with* the grain. The teeth are chisel edged to shave off the fibres of the grain. The large gullet carries the sawdust out of the kerf. **B.** Cross cut saw. 24in. to 26in. long (610mm to 661mm) with 6, 7 or 8 ppi. The saw is used to cut across the grain on hardwoods and softwoods and for working with the grain on very hardwoods. The knife point shaped teeth gives the sharper cut needed when working across the grain. **C.** Panel saw. 20in. to 22in. long (508mm to 558mm) with 10 ppi. The panel saw is used for fine cross cut and jointing work and for cutting plywood, blockboard and hardboard. The teeth are a similar shape to those of a cross cut saw.

Fig.2. Double sided saw for cutting greenwood. One side is fine toothed for cutting slender plants and the other has large open gullets to carry away sawdust when cutting larger timber. It is usually Teflon coated to stop it sticking in sappy greenwood.

Fig.3. Tenon or back saw. 8in. to 14in. long with 13, 14, 15, 16 or 20 ppi. It is used for jointing and for cutting across the grain on small pieces. The back may be brass or steel. The saw with 20 ppi is for cutting dovetails. Its blade is

thin to give greater accuracy. All cuts made with a dovetail saw should be along the grain as it performs a ripping action.

Fig.4. A. Saw knife or pad saw with a keyhole blade. **B.** Metal keyhole saw blade. Both are used for cutting small irregular shapes in the middle of a board.

Fig.5. Flooring saw. 6 to 10 ppi. The rounded nose allows you to cut into floorboards without damaging adjacent boards.

Fig.6. General purpose saw. The teeth are hardened and tempered. It is used for cutting wood laminates, plastic, mild steel, rubber, asbestos etc. It is a handy odd job tool but is not recommended for first class, accurate work. The handle is adjustable to enable work in awkward places and positions.

Fig.7. Coping saw. It has very fine teeth and is used for cutting tight curves. Tension is applied to the replaceable blade by tightening the handle.

Fig.8. Fret or piercing saw. It is similar to coping saw but is deeper to allow work with larger boards. There are many types of blade available, the choice depending on what material you wish to cut.

Fig.9 Junior hack saw. General purpose saw for light metal work.

Fig.10. Adjustable frame hack saw. It can take 10in. to 12in. (254mm to 305mm) blades. Blades are available in range of ppi from 14 to 32.

Fig.11. Sheet saw. This is available with 12in. (305mm) blade with 14 to 32 ppi for cutting metal or 16in. (407mm) blade with 6, 10 or 14 ppi for cutting thicker building material such as asbestos cement, insulation slabs and metal covered plywood. It is more accurate for cutting straight lines than general purpose saw.

NELSON HARGREAVES

DATA SHEET

Cramping and clamping tools

Accurate carpentry, especially the sawing or planing of timber, depends on holding the workpiece in a steady position. Also, one of the last stages in all carpentry projects, that of assembling the components, requires the application of sufficient pressure to push the pieces together. This DATA SHEET illustrates the common clamping tools—those that hold workpieces firmly—and cramping tools—those that force com-

ponents together. This brief guide to cramping techniques enables you to make a really efficient job of your projects.

1. Woodworker's vice. This can either be fixed permanently to a work bench (as in 14) or may be fitted with a simple cramping device to allow temporary fixing to a table. This model is shown here. Jaw widths vary from 4in. (100mm) to 10½in. (263mm).

2. Sash cramp. This is used for cramping large, regular-shaped objects such as doors and window frames. These cramps are available in the simple rectangle (shown here), light T-bar, and strong T-bar sections. Working lengths vary from 24in. (610mm) to 84in. (2.1m).

3. Lengthening bar for a sash cramp. This is used for extending the working length of a sash cramp. Available in lengths ranging from 24in. (610mm) to 60in. (1.5m).

4. Mechanic's vice. This sturdily built vice will withstand heavy hammering. Use fibre jaws with the vice when holding soft metals. This type of vice is also available with a swivel base and comes with jaw widths ranging between 2½in. (63mm) and 8in. (200mm).

5. Corner or mitre cramp. This is used for holding two mitred pieces of timber at right angles to each other while they are pinned or glued—particularly useful in the construction of pictures and other frames. Some mitre cramps have a device which guides a tenon or back saw cut to give a reasonably accurate 45° mitre.

6 and 6A. Heavy duty and medium duty G or C cramp. This is the most common portable holding tool. Available in jaw openings ranging from 2in. (50mm) to 18in. (457mm).

7. Deep throat G or C cramp. Available in jaw openings of between 2in. (50mm) and 4in. (100mm).

8. Bench holdfast. A very quick action holding device which drops into metal collars fixed into the bench surface at convenient points. Maximum openings range from 6⅞in. (172mm) to 9in. (225mm).

9. Quick action cramp. This is probably the most useful all-round cramp, but it is not as readily available from tool stores as the G cramp.

10. Cramp heads. These are used in conjunction with a length of hardwood batten with fixing holes drilled through it. This tool is a cheap, but less stable, alternative to the sash cramp.

11. Universal gripping and clamping wrench. This adjustable wrench can be set by means of a knurled adjusting screw to grip or lock at a pre-set jaw width. It is available under several trade names including Mole and Grip-Lok.

12. Edging cramp. This tool is particularly useful for fixing laminate or timber edging strip to narrow sections. Available in 2in. (50mm), 2½in. (63mm) and 3in. (75mm) working openings.

13. Web clamp. This is a very versatile tool which can be used for cramping irregular-shaped pieces as well as regular-shaped items.

14. Carpenter's front vice. See 1.

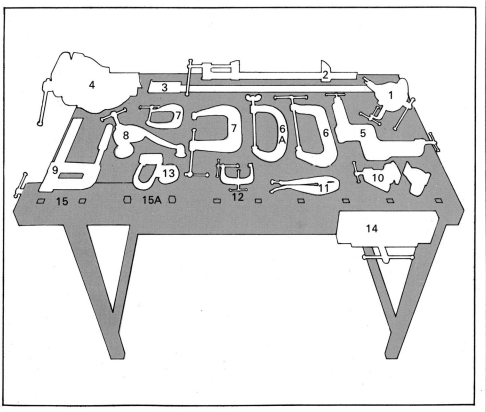

DATA SHEET

Spanners and wrenches

Do-it-yourself repairs to plumbing and other pipework usually involves disconnection of some part of the system. For this you will need shifting tools—wrenches and spanners. This DATA SHEET lists the tools that are used for specific jobs and also describes some of the pliers available for electrical work and other jobs involving the use of metal wire.

1. Socket set. Some of the accessories used with the socket set are the tee bar wrench (2), the rachet handle (3) and the extension bar (4). Sockets are available in the following thread styles:—American Fine (AF), British Standard Whitworth (BSW), Iso metric (M) and British Association (BA). Sockets for the last thread style are very small. These tools are used for loosening nuts and, providing you use the right size socket, the tool will not slip. There is, therefore, less chance of damaging the head of the nut than with a spanner. You can also achieve greater torque, or circular force, with these tools than with a spanner. Other accessories for the socket set (not shown) are speed braces and the universal joint. These allow the sockets to be used in awkward positions. A torque wrench (not shown) can be calibrated to allow nuts or bolts to be tightened to a specific pressure. Socket sets are fairly expensive to buy but, as with most of the tools shown here, they can usually be hired.

2. Tee bar wrench.

3. Rachet handle.

4. Extension bar.

5 and 6. Pipe wrenches. These types of pipe wrench are available in lengths ranging from 6in. (150mm) to 48in. (1000mm) and will cope with pipe sizes ranging from ½in. (13mm) to 6in. (150mm) diameter. These wrenches are mainly used for work on iron pipes—they can easily damage softer metals like copper and brass. The head is sprung loaded and this, together with the toothed jaws, enables a strong grip to be exerted on round pipe sections as opposed to hexagonal nut sections.

7. Adjustable wrench or spanner. This is a very useful tool, particularly for copper plumbing. They are available in a range of lengths from 4in. (100mm) to 20in. (500mm) with jaw opening of between ½in. (13mm) to 2½in. (63mm). Do not use this wrench on fine engineering nuts or bolts of the type used, for example, for automobile assembly. The jaws are too large for such nuts which can easily be damaged—and this could result in the loosening of these nuts and bolts and the creation of a potentially dangerous situation.

An easy reference guide to the key diagram.
1. Socket set 2. Tee bar wrench 3. Rachet handle 4. Extension bar 5 and 6. Pipe wrenches 7. Adjustable wrench or spanner 8. Chain wrench 9. Universal gripping and clamping tool 10. Slip joint pliers 11. Electrician's or combination square nosed pliers. 13. Round nosed pliers 14. Water pump pliers 15. Scotch gas pliers 16. Open ended spanners and wrenches 17. Ring spanners 18. Combination spanners 19. Allen keys or hollow head wrenches

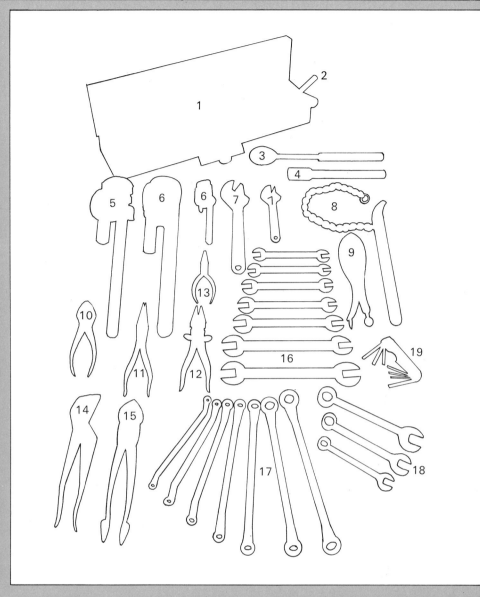

8. Chain wrench. This is an easily adjustable wrench for shifting heavily rusted or encrusted iron pipe joints. It is lighter to use though less effective than the heavy duty pipe wrench. Available in handle lengths of between 12in. (300mm) and 18in. (450mm).

9. Universal gripping and clamping tool. This tool has a variety of trade names including Mole and Grip-lok. Available in a wide variety of shapes and sizes. An attachment is available which allows the tool to be used as a mini bench vice.

10. Slip joint pliers. This tool has a thin section to allow the nose to reach into tight places. It has two jaw opening positions and a shear type wire cutter.

11. Needle nosed side cutting pliers. These are used for fine wire work. Radio pliers are the same except that they have insulated handles.

12. Electrician's or combination square nosed pliers. These are heavy duty pliers with a square nose and serated hole—both of which can be used for holding small diameter tubing and nuts and bolts. Usually this tool has two types of wire cutter, a shear cutter and a side cutter. The handles are insulated but make sure when you buy this tool that the handles are guaranteed to withstand any voltage with which the pliers are likely to come into contact.

13. Round nosed pliers. These pliers do not have a great deal of domestic application but they are useful for coiling or twisting wire.

14. Water pump pliers. These are adjustable pliers with up to six different jaw positions. They are general purpose pliers useful in plumbing.

15. Scotch gas pliers. These are general purpose pliers, used where a light but firm grip is needed.

16. Open ended spanners and wrenches. These are available in every nut and thread size encountered.

17. Ring spanners. It is preferable to use these spanners wherever possible as they are far less likely to slip than open ended spanners. You can also obtain greater torque with these spanners.

18. Combination spanners. These tools have an open spanner at one end and a ring spanner at the other. For a complete set you will obviously need twice as many spanners than for a full set of ring or open ended spanners.

19. Allen keys or hollow head wrenches. These are used with hexagonal hollow headed screws.

Note: There is a wide variety of pliers and spanners available. Only the most common are shown here.

DATA SHEET

Measuring and marking tools

Accurate and efficient measuring and marking is a must for nearly all DIY jobs – without this, furniture, windows, floors and similar pieces you repair might not fit together properly. This DATA SHEET lists the wide variety of measuring and marking tools available, and tells you about their general and specific uses.

The procedure for marking off distances on timber and metal is straightforward, but a strict adherence to the basic requirements will make for accurate working—and save you time in the long run.

When measuring and marking timber or metal you must work from a squared edge or line. To square a line across timber, you have to cut two edges of the timber—the face edge and the face side—square. Plane two edges square, checking for this periodically with a try square (**24** in the DATA SHEET) and then mark them for later identification. Sight along the length of the edge being planed with a straightedge such as a steel rule (**25**).

If you wish to mark a line parallel to the long edge of a fairly narrow piece of timber, a marking gauge (**9**) will do the job. If the timber is wide—a man-made board, for example—measure the required width across the face side from the face edge at both ends of the board. Use a folding rule (**28**) laid on its edge for this. Mark the distances with a pencil and then join up the marks with a straightedge.

To square a line at right angles to the face edge lay the blade of a try square across the face side. Use a marking knife (one example is shown in **18**) to score the timber, using the blade of the try square to guide the mark. Then fill in the scored lines with a carpenter's pencil (**27**), held against a steel rule (**25**) or try square.

If you wish to cut through the timber at this point, rather than simply measure from the squared line, continue the squared line around all four surfaces of the piece.

Marking and squaring off a required distance on metal is basically the same process though, of course, the metal edges have to be filed or ground rather than planed square. Use the engineer's square (**23**) and the steel rule (**25**) to check for this. To square lines across metal use a scriber (**17** and **18**) and an engineer's square. The marked lines will show up better if the metal is coated with engineer's blue (**5**) before scribing.

1. Glazier's tee square and lath. These are used for the direct scoring of glass with a cutter held against the tee square. These tools are also useful for marking out large man-made boards. Squares are available in 36in., 60in. and 72in. (1m, 1.5m and 2m) sizes. Laths come in lengths of 36in., 60in., 72in. and 120in. (1m, 1.5m, 2m and 3m).

2. Chalk snap line and can of chalk. The chalk snap line is used for marking straight lines on both horizontal and vertical surfaces. The line is held at both ends and plucked in the middle—this leaves a chalk line on the surface. The snap line shown here can be filled with powdered chalk from a can (also shown). With other types, the line is rubbed with a solid piece of chalk.

3. Roofing square. This is a right angled steel square calibrated to allow all the angles necessary for roof construction to be easily marked. Instructions for using the tool are supplied by the manufacturer and once these are mastered the roofing square is invaluable in building carpentry. It can also be used for squaring up large carcasses such as wardrobe frames.

4. Plumb bob and line. This is used for testing verticals and it can also be used as a chalk snap line.

5. Engineer's blue. This is coated on metal to allow marked lines to show up more clearly. Available in either liquid form (shown here) or as a paste—the former is the easier to use.

6. Builder's line and pegs. This is used for checking the levels of brick courses. The pins are knocked into mortar course and a line level (**21**) hung on the string.

7. Boat level. This spirit level is used for checking horizontals and verticals on all small jobs.

8. Spirit level. This spirit level is used to check horizontal and vertical surfaces on larger pieces of work. Some levels have an adjustable glass for checking angles.

9. Mortise gauge. This is used to mark one or more lines on a piece of timber, parallel to one edge of that timber. Its specific use is for marking out for mortise and tenon joints but it can be used as an ordinary marking gauge (not shown).

10. Trammel heads. These are scribing points which are attached to a bar or batten between ¾in. (19mm) and 1½in. (38mm) thick. They are used for marking out large radii and curves.

11. Surface gauge. The marking part of this tool consists of a scriber with a hardened point that can be set at any position on the vertical spindle of the tool. The spindle, in turn, can be set at any angle you require. The scriber is used to mark a line on metal parallel to the base of the tool.

12. Outside calipers. These are used for measuring the external diameter of circular or

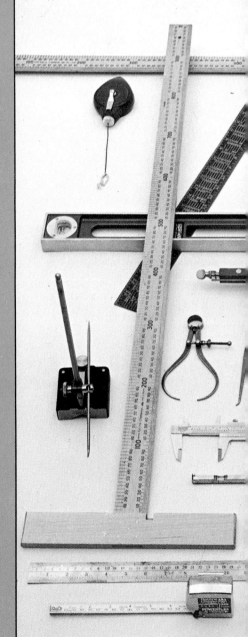

1. Glazier's tee square and lath. 2. Chalk snap line and can of chalk. 3. Roofing square. 4. Plumb bob and line. 5. Engineer's blue. 6. Builder's line and pegs. 7. Boat level. 8. Spirit level. 9. Mortise gauge. 10. Trammel heads. 11. Surface gauge. 12. Outside calipers. 13. Inside calipers. 14. Dividers. 15. Centre punches. 16. Automat...

irregularly shaped items. The range of sizes goes from a 2in. (50mm) maximum opening to a 3ft (915mm) maximum opening. The larger sizes are commonly used by sculptors and potters.

13. Inside calipers. These are used to measure internal diameters.

14. Dividers. This tool has hardened ground points and is used for stepping out odd measurements and scribing circles on metal. Sizes range from 5in. (125mm) maximum opening to 12in.

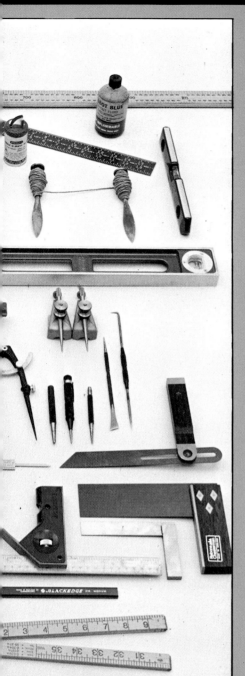

the tool can be adjusted within the range of approximately 5lb (2.2kg) for light punching to about 30lb (13kg) for heavy punching.

17. Universal scriber and marking knife. One end of this tool is sharpened to a point for scribing metal and the other end is ground to a chisel shaped cutting edge for marking wood.

18. Engineer's scriber. This is used with a steel rule and square for marking metal.

19. Vernier caliper gauge. This is a very accurate calibrated gauge for measuring internal and external diameters.

20. Sliding bevel. This tool is used for setting out angles, or bevels. Available in blade sizes of 9in. or 230mm, 10½in. or 270mm and 12in. or 300mm.

21. Line level. This is used with a builder's line (**6**). When using the tool the line must be as taut as possible. Not a particularly accurate tool, the line level is used mainly as a guide.

22. Combination try and mitre square. This is used for marking angles and mitres. The blade, along which the stock slides, is calibrated in either metric or imperial measurements, or both.

23. Engineer's square. This is used for marking right angles across metal. The stock is hardened steel—this is so that rough metal edges do not damage the tool.

24. Carpenter's square. This is used for setting out right angles and for testing edges when planing timber square. The blade of the tool is sprung steel and the stock is protected by a thin strip of brass or other soft metal. These squares are available with 4½in. or 115mm, 6in. or 150mm, 7½in. or 190mm, 9in. or 230mm and 12in. or 300mm blades.

25. Steel rule. These range from 6in. or 150mm to 3ft (900mm) lengths. They are accurately calibrated for fine work.

26. Adjustable steel tape. The pocket size variety, when fully extended, range in length from 6ft (1.83m) to 12ft (3.66m). The larger varieties are available in either steel, fabric or glassfibre in lengths up to 100ft (30.5mm).

27. Carpenter's pencil. This has an oblong shaped lead which is sharpened to a chisel edge so that it can be used to black-in scribed lines.

28. Folding boxwood rule. This tool is also available in plastic. Primarily for joinery and carpentry use, it should be used narrow edge onto the timber for accurate marking. These rules are available in 2ft or 600mm and 3ft or 1m sizes.

centre punch. **17.** *Universal scriber and marking knife.* **18.** *Engineer's scriber.* **19.** *Vernier caliper gauge.* **20.** *Sliding bevel.* **21.** *Line level.* **22.** *Combination try & mitre square.* **23.** *Engineer's square.* **24.** *Carpenter's square.* **25.** *Steel rule.* **26.** *Adjustable steel tape.* **27.** *Carpenter's pencil.* **28.** *Folding boxwood rule.*

NELSON HARGREAVES

(300mm) maximum opening.

15. Centre punches. A fine centre punch is shown towards the right of the photograph, a coarse centre punch towards the left. These are used for spot marking metal to give a guide for drilling. The point is marked by tapping the wide end of the tool with a hammer.

16. Automatic centre punch. This centre punch is spring loaded so you do not have to tap the end with a hammer. Spring pressure of

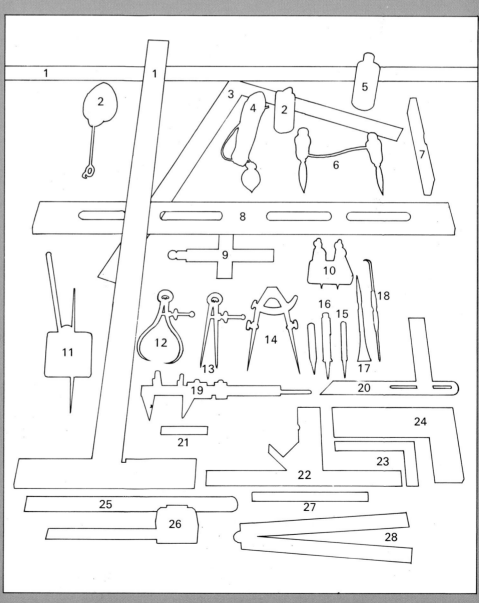

DATA SHEET

Carpenter's basic tool kit

NELSON HARGREAVES

There is a vast range of tools on the market to cope with all DIY jobs. Many of these have very specific uses. A collection of basic tools is, however, quite sufficient for most requirements. This DATA SHEET presents a basic tool kit for the home carpenter.

1. Tenon or back saw. These saws are available in blade lengths of between 8in. and 14in. (203mm and 355mm) with 13, 14, 15, 16 or 20 points. This is used for jointing and cutting across the grain on small pieces. The back of the blade may be of brass or steel. The saw with 20 points is for cutting dovetails and it has a thin blade to give greater accuracy. The dovetail saw performs a ripping action, so cut along the grain when using it.

2. Hand saw. This is used for cutting larger pieces of timber. There are three types of handsaw. The one shown here is a panel saw. It is 20in. to 22in. (508 to 558mm) long with 10 points. Its specialist purpose is for fine cross cut and jointing work and for cutting plywood, blockboard and hardboard. The other types of handsaw (not shown) are the rip saw and the cross cut saw. The rip saw is 26in. (661mm) long with 5 points. Its specialist purpose is for cutting softwoods, working with the grain. The cross cut saw is 24in. to 26in. (610mm to 661mm) long with 6, 7 or 8 points and is specially used for cutting across the grain of hardwoods and softwoods and for working with the grain on very hardwoods.

3. G cramps. These are used for a range of cramping purposes. These cramps are available in a 1in. to 18in. (25mm to 457mm) range of opening and between 1in. to 8in. (25mm to 203mm) depth of throat. When using G cramps always place a waste scrap of timber between the piece to be cramped and the shoes of the cramps. This prevents bruising of the piece.

4. Rachet brace. This has spring loaded jaws in a screw tightened chuck. It is specially designed for holding wood auger bits (**5**). The brace is available with or without a reversible rachet in a sweep (the arc described by the turning handle of the brace) ranging from 5$\frac{7}{8}$in. (148mm) to 14in. (355mm).

5. Wood auger bits. These are used with **4**.

6. Hand drill. This is used for holding wood and metal twist drill bits (**7**) and countersink or rose bits (**8**). The example shown here has a double pinion (cogged drive wheel).

7. Twist bits. These are commonly available in sizes ranging from $\frac{1}{64}$in. to $\frac{1}{2}$in. (13mm). The type of steel used depends on the use to which the bit is to be put.

8. Countersink or rose bit. This is used for countersinking drilled holes so that countersunk screw heads will fit flush with the surface of the piece you are working with.

9. Warrington pattern or cross pein hammer. This is used for general nailing and joinery and can be used for planishing and beating metal. Weights of these hammers range from 6oz (170g) to 16oz (450g).

10. Claw hammer. This is used for general purpose carpentry, in particular, for driving and removing nails. When taking out nails, make sure that the nail head is well into the claw of the hammer and, if it is necessary to protect the surface of the wood, place a scrap piece of timber between the claw and the wood. Exert even pressure to lever the nail out. Claw hammers are available in weights ranging from 16oz (450g) to 24oz (570g).

11. Carpenter's or joiner's mallet. This is used for general carpentry and cabinet work and is available in head lengths of between 4in. (100mm) and 5$\frac{1}{2}$in. (180mm).

12. Handyman's knife. This useful carpentry knife can be fitted with a variety of blades to suit specific purposes. The blades include angled concave, convex, linoleum and hooked blades. Wood and metal saw blades (**12A** and **12B**) can also be fitted to this tool as can a blade for cutting plastic laminate.

13. Bench plane. There are various types of bench plane and they are available in a range of lengths and widths. The smooth plane (shown here) comes in lengths of between 9$\frac{1}{2}$in. and 10$\frac{1}{4}$in. (241mm to 260mm) and widths of between 1$\frac{3}{4}$in. and 2$\frac{3}{8}$in. (44mm to 60mm). The Jack plane (not shown) is available in lengths of between 14in. (356mm) and 15in. (381mm) and widths ranging from 2in. (50mm) to 2$\frac{3}{8}$in. (60mm). The Fore plane (not shown) is 18in. (457mm) long and 2$\frac{3}{8}$in. (60mm) wide. The Jointer or Try plane (not shown) is 22in. (561mm) long and 2$\frac{3}{8}$in. (60mm) wide. When working with resinuous or sticky woods, a plane with a longtitudinally corrugated sole makes the job of planing easier because friction between the timber and the plane is reduced. If you do not have such a plane, apply a spot of vegetable oil to the sole of your ordinary plane—this will perform much the same function.

14. Surform plane. This is one of a range of open rasp/planing tools, all of which are useful and versatile. They are primarily used for rough work but with care some reasonably fine craftmanship can be produced. Each tool in this range has replaceable blades.

15. Block plane. This small plane is particularly useful for fine cabinet work and for planing end grain. Available in lengths of between 6in. and 7in. (152mm to 178mm) and cutter widths of between 1$\frac{15}{16}$in. (49mm) and 1$\frac{5}{8}$in. (41mm).

16. Sliding bevel. This tool is used for setting out angles, or bevels. Available in blade sizes of 9in. (230mm), 10$\frac{1}{2}$in. (270mm) and 12in. (300mm).

17. Bradawl. This is a chisel pointed boring tool used for marking screw positions and counterboring for small size screws.

18. Adjustable steel rule. The pocket size variety, when fully extended, range in length from 6ft (1.83m) to 12ft (3.66m). The larger varieties are available in either steel, glassfibre or fabric in lengths of up to 100ft (30.5m).

19. Carpenter's square. This is used for setting out right angles and for testing edges when planing timber square. The tool has a sprung steel blade and the stock is protected by a thin strip of brass or other soft metal. Available in blade lengths of 4$\frac{1}{2}$in. (115mm), 7$\frac{1}{2}$in. (190mm), 9in. (230mm) and 12in. (300mm).

20. Marking gauge. This is used to mark one or more lines on a piece of timber, parallel to one edge of that timber. The type shown here is a mortise gauge which has a fixed point on one side and one fixed and one adjustable point on the other. Its specific use is for marking out mortise and tenon joints but it can be used in the same way as an ordinary marking gauge.

21. Folding boxwood rule. This tool is also available in plastic. Primarily for joinery and carpentry use, it should be used narrow edge onto the timber for the most accurate marking. These rules are available in 2ft (600mm) and 3ft (1m) sizes.

22. Scriber marking knife. One end of this tool is ground to a chisel shaped cutting edge for marking timber. The other end is sharpened to a point and can be used for scribing metal.

23. Nail punch or set. This tool is used for tapping pin and nail heads below the surface of timber. A range of head sizes is available to suit pin and nail sizes.

24. Centre punch. This is used for spot marking metal to give a guide for drilling. The point is marked by tapping the wide end of the tool with a hammer. Automatic centre punches (not shown) are available. These are spring loaded so you do not have to tap the end of the tool.

25. Carpenter's pencil. This has an oblong shaped lead which is sharpened to a chisel edge so that it can be used to black in lines scribed on timber.

26. Pozidriv type screwdriver. This tip is designed for use with Pozidriv type screws which are increasingly replacing screws with the conventional blade head. The Pozidriv screw head allows far greater contact between the screwdriver tip and the screw head—providing, of course that the correct size of screwdriver tip is used. This makes for greater torque (twisting power) and reduces the likelihood of tool slip and consequent damage to the work.

27. Cabinet screwdriver. This tool is available in blade lengths of between 3in. (75mm) and 18in. (457mm) and tip widths of between $\frac{3}{16}$in. (4.8mm) to $\frac{1}{2}$in. (13mm). The screwdriver tip should fit the screw slot completely and the risk of tool slip will be further reduced if the screwdriver tip has been cross ground.

28. Carpenter's chisels. These are available in several shapes and sizes of both handles and

blades. The firmer bevel edge chisels shown here are probably the most useful all round chisels to have in a basic tool kit. Chisel handles are either of ash, boxwood or plastic (shown here). Plastic handles are virtually unbreakable on quality chisels but timber handles should be treated with care and should only be hit with a wooden mallet. Blade widths vary from $\frac{1}{8}$in. (3mm) to 2in. (50mm).

29. Oilstones. These are used for sharpening the cutting edges of such tools as planes and chisels. There are two main kinds of oilstone, natural and artificial. Natural stone comes in several types. *Washita* gives a good finish and cuts well. *Arkansas* is an expensive stone but it is of high quality and produces a very fine edge. These are the most commonly used natural oilstones. Artificial stones come in three grades—coarse, medium and fine—and have the advantage of maintaining their quality. They are available in a selection of sizes including 5in. x 2in. (125mm x 50mm), 6in. x 2in. (150mm x 50mm), 8in. x 2in. (200mm x 50mm),

10in. x 2in. (250mm x 50mm) and 8in. x 1$\frac{7}{8}$in. (200mm x 45mm).

30. Fine machine oil. This has many lubricating uses in the workshop and is a reasonable substitute for Neatsfoot oil when using an oilstone.

31. Honing gauge. This is a useful device for holding bladed tools at the correct angle for sharpening on an oilstone. The disadvantage of this tool is that it tends to cause wear in the centre of the oilstone rather than distributing the wear evenly over the whole stone.

32. Junior hacksaw. This is a general purpose saw for light metalworking jobs.

33. Shoulder pincers. These are used for pulling nails and pins from timber. If possible, always place a scrap of waste timber between the jaws of the pincers and the work piece to avoid bruising.

34. Slip joint pliers. This tool has a thin section so that the jaws can reach into tight places. It has two jaw opening positions and shear type wire cutter.

DATA SHEET

Bricklaying tools

Bricklaying is one of the most basic construction jobs and one which you can do easily. But you need to know what the essential tools and materials are—and what specialist equipment is available to help you do a really professional job.

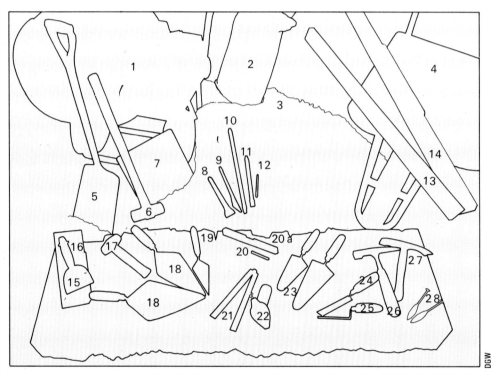

The preparatory work for bricklaying is all important. In particular, you must ensure that you get the first course of bricks level—if you don't the whole wall will be out of true. To get the first course level, tie a line (22) to two bricks and stretch it taut. Hook a line level (20) on to this line to make sure it is level. Lay the first course of bricks on concrete, level with this line and check the course with a long spirit level (13). Subsequent courses are kept level by tying the line between pins (28) which are knocked into a suitable mortar course.

1. Barrow-mix concrete mixer. Hiring a mixer is worthwhile if you have a fairly big job to do. The mixer tilts so the concrete can be emptied straight into a wheelbarrow and taken to the site.

2 and 3. Cement and sand. The different grades of cement and sand can be mixed in various proportions, together with gravel, for particular uses.

4. Wheelbarrow. A pneumatic tyre makes for easier working. As with other tools make sure you clean it immediately after use—especially if you have been carrying concrete.

5. Square mouth shovel. Shovels are available in various sizes and shapes—including round, square and taper mouth shovels. You must scrub your shovel after use.

6. Sledge hammer. Used for breaking up hardcore and for demolition work.

7. Hawk. Used for carrying plaster and mortar and for holding it close to the work.

8. Mason's pitching tool. Used for cutting, splitting and trimming stone.

9. Plugging chisel. Used for chasing out mortar courses and for making holes in brickwork prior to plugging.

10, 11 and 12. Cold chisels. The length of cold chisels varies between 4in. and 18in. with a $\frac{1}{4}$in to 1in. cutting edge. The larger types are used for cutting holes through, and for shaping bricks. The smaller chisels are used for cutting holes in stoneware drain pipes when jointing them with a saddle.

13. Long spirit level. About 32in. long and used for checking horizontal and vertical levels. At the start of construction it is used for setting building lines and these should be checked regularly afterwards with the level. Always clean the tool after using it on concrete or it will not be accurate.

14. Feather-edge. A home made tool, used to give straight lines when pointing. Pointing can be done either with the bevel edge part of this tool or with a trowel (see 19 and 25).

15. Brick bolster. Used for cutting bricks and for knocking through. Bolsters have 3in. to $4\frac{1}{2}$in. wide blades and can be bought with a rubber grip on the handle.

16. Bat gauge. A self made tool which is a quick measure of $\frac{1}{2}$ and $\frac{3}{4}$ bats, (part of a brick).

NELSON HARGREAVES

The gauge should be made of hardwood.

17. Club hammer. Used with a bolster for cutting bricks and knocking through. The weight varies from 2½lb to 4lb.

18. Broad heel brick trowels. Used for laying mortar and cutting bricks. Trowels are left or right handed. One edge is hardened and this is used to cut bricks using a back hand action. The other edge is used for smoothing on mortar.

19. Pointing trowel. These can be used instead of a feather-edge for pointing. It produces a sloping face on the mortar course and rain water drains more readily from the brickwork.

20. Line level. A small spirit level that is hooked

onto a chalked snap line to check whether it is level.

20A. Torpedo or boat level. A spirit level suitable for use in confined spaces—such as at the corner of a newly started wall set in a trench when building foundations.

21. 3ft or 1m folding boxwood rule.

22. Chalk line and chalk. This is tied between pins (28) and used as a snap line. It ensures that brick courses are level. This version can also be used as a plumb line.

23. Gauging trowels. These are used for long, narrow work or for general work The whole blade is hardened.

24. Mastic or window trowel. This is used for applying cement, putty or mastic up the sides of window frames or in other small gaps. The blade is 6in. long, ¼in. to 1in. wide and has parallel edges.

25. Brick jointer. This has a curved edge and is used for hollow pointing.

26. Brick hammer. This has a square, hardened face and cutting edge.

27. Scutch or comb hammer. This is used for trimming and cutting hard bricks that would damage a trowel. The combs are replaceable.

28. Pins. These are knocked into a mortar course and a chalk line tied between them.

DATA SHEET

Equipment for upholstery

The tools and equipment used in upholstery are simple but specialized and, although it is possible to improvise many of them, it is worth buying the proper things if you plan a large project. Here are the most common items you need.

This page, from right to left

Webbing is the basis for most upholstery, and it is tacked in inter-woven strands across the frame to support the padding. It is essential that it is stretched taut, and for this a web strainer (shown with the webbing) is used. (Details on using the strainer were given in HOME FABRICS 57.)

Tacks are used to attach the various materials to the frame (nails should never be used because these could damage it). The $\frac{3}{8}$in. fine tacks (bottom) are for fabrics, and the $\frac{5}{8}$in. improved (above), which have a large head, are for webbing and spring canvas, both of which take a lot of pressure.

Tape measures are one of the few items common to other fields of sewing, and are used to measure off pieces of fabric, etc.

Shears, which are really sharp, are essential for cutting out fabric and making notches.

Mallet and **ripping chisel** are needed for lifting the heads of tacks when removing old upholstery. The tip of the chisel is blunt to prevent damaging the frame, and should always be driven in the direction of the grain. (More details about this were given in HOME FABRICS 34).

Tack lifter (second from bottom) is for pulling out the tacks once the heads have been lifted. Alternatively, you can use the claw end of the hammer.

Cabriole hammers (bottom) are quite different from regular carpenters' hammers because they usually have two small heads ($\frac{1}{4}$in. and $\frac{5}{8}$in.). They are very heavy so that they drive in the tacks quickly and without damaging the frame from continual or direct blows. Sometimes the hammer may have one head ($\frac{5}{8}$in.) and a claw for lifting tacks.

Upholsterers' needles are much heavier and longer (10in.-12in.) than regular sewing

needles and are pointed at both ends so that the needle can be inserted into thick stuffing with one end, and pulled out in another place with the other end. It is mainly used with twine (top left) for making a stitched edge. (For further details about this, see HOME FABRICS 57).

Regulators have one pointed end and one blunt, rounded end. The point is for distributing the stuffing evenly and for forming a roll edge. The blunt end is for pushing fabric into the 'crevices' at the back uprights of a chair, and for forming pleats in deep buttoning.

This page, from left to right

Rubberized webbing is a more recent introduction to upholstery and, because it is resilient, it combines the functions of regular webbing and springs in some cases. It is best used with foam rubber as the padding. (Further details about it were given in HOME FABRICS 34).

Coil springs are the traditional form of springing, and are available in different sizes and gauges. The heavier, larger springs are for the seats of easy chairs; the lighter, smaller ones are for the back and arms of easy chairs and for dining chair seats.

Sisal is used to lash springs together to prevent them from moving about in the seat and also to set them at the right height and angle. Laid cord is also used for this, but is much more expensive.

Spring units, which are pre-formed, are often used in mass-produced furniture because they are quicker and cheaper than individual coil springs which have to be attached by hand. With units, the springs are held together by a wire mesh and metal strips are used instead of webbing. The disadvantages of these units are that they are available in a limited range of sizes and they tend to squeak when sat on.

Zig-zag springs and **tension springs** (foreground) are also put in smaller, modern chairs. Like rubber webbing, they span the frame in one direction only—usually across, rather than from front to back—and are fixed to the side rails. They are easy to use and are popular because they give a shallower, lighter seat than is possible with coil springs.

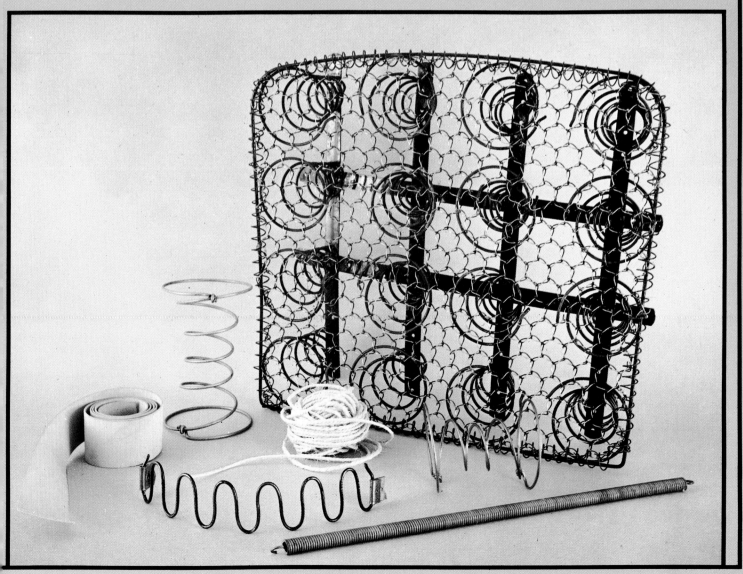

First-aid for fabrics

In every household from time to time you are liable to find stains in fabrics which will not come out with normal laundering. You can, however, normally remove them with some other treatment.

Always try to treat a stain immediately it happens, because it will be much easier to remove while it is still on the surface of the fabric than when it has penetrated it fully.

Non-greasy marks should be rinsed with plain cold water, greasy marks dusted with talcum powder or french chalk. Spread salt over a wine or fruit mark—this will not remove it, but will help to prevent it spreading.

Types of stains

Most stains fall into one of four categories, and those in each are usually treated in a similar way (see below). These are :

Protein stains, such as blood, egg, milk.
Vegetable stains, such as wine, fruit juice, cocoa, tea, coffee.
Grease stains, such as fat, hair and suntan oil,

Above. Spilt coffee is a common occurrence, and need not leave a stain if treated immediately. But even if it does, there are chemicals which will remove it.

lipstick.
Paint stains, all types of paint and nail varnish.

The equipment

Various chemicals can be used to remove stains, and it is a good idea to keep these in the house. For safety, they should always be clearly labelled and, if there are children about, they should be put in a high cupboard which can be locked. You also need cotton wool for applying the chemical and some blotting paper and old sheeting to make a pad.

Acetone, which is derived from petroleum, is a powerful solvent for nail varnish, fats, plastics and some adhesives. It can be used on all fabrics except acetates which it will dissolve. Amyl acetate may be used where acetone would damage the fabric.

Ammonia is a mild alkali which is useful for

removing acid stains. It should be used in a solution of 1 tablespoon to 1 pint (0.5 litre) of warm water. If the colour is affected, it should be neutralized immediately with a weak solution of white vinegar and water, and then rinsed.

Benzene, a colourless liquid which smells of coal tar, is a solvent for rubber, paint, tar and oils. It can be used on most fabrics and should not affect the colour.

Bleach can be used to remove stains from white cotton and linens which have not been treated in any way for crease and shrink resistance. Chlorine bleaches (sodium hypochlorite) should never be used on coloured fabrics, silk, wool, nylon or synthetic fibres.

The strength of these bleaches varies according to the brand, and so the manufacturer's instructions should be followed. They should never be used in the same water as a biological washing powder, because they will destroy the powder's enzymes.

A different sort of bleach, sodium hydrosulphite, can be used on fabrics other than cotton and linen, but again it will remove the colour.

Dygon, which is often used to remove the colour from fabrics before re-dyeing, is based on this.

Carbon tetrachloride is a good solvent for grease marks, but it should be used with great care because inhalation of its fumes can be poisonous. It must be used in a well ventilated room or preferably outside, and fabrics treated with it must not be ironed until completely dry or dangerous vapours may form.

Use it neat and apply with cotton wool. Place the fabric, stain-side down, on to a clean fabric pad or blotting paper. Apply the carbon tetrachloride in a large ring round the stain and work inwards. Move the pad underneath as soon as it becomes soiled.

Borax is a mild alkali which can be used for acid stains and for fire-proofing fabrics. For a solvent, it should be used in a solution of 1oz (28gr) to 1 pint (0.5 litre) of water. The fabric is soaked in the solution, then rinsed and washed.

Eucalyptus oil is ideal for removing tar and oil marks. It can be used on most fabrics by placing a pad underneath the mark, rubbing the oil well into the stain with cotton wool on the wrong side.

Methylated spirit is good for marks from grass, seaweed, perfume and ballpoint pens, and will also remove french polish and wax stains.

Soda (sodium carbonate) dissolves alkali and grease marks. When it is dissolved in hot water, it is effective in a few minutes. It can also be used to remove sea-water marks from leather by dissolving it in milk for half an hour.

Turpentine, or turpentine substitute, is used for removing paint, varnish and enamel stains, and is also good for cleaning baths.

Glycerine, which is a by-product of soap manufacture, is a good solvent for obstinate vegetable stains and other marks from substances which are water-soluble. It can be used on all types of fabric, but it must be rinsed out thoroughly with water because it might leave a mark.

Oxalic acid can be used to treat ink, rust and iron mould, and old vegetable stains. It is poisonous, and should be used with great care. The crystals should be dissolved in the proportion 1 teaspoon to ¾pt. (0.4 litre) of warm water.

A warning

Many of these chemicals are either toxic, giving off dangerous vapours, or inflammable, and sometimes both. It is essential, therefore, to make it a rule to use them in a well-ventilated room or preferably outside, never to inhale them or to use them near a naked light. Never smoke while you are using them.

Always test the chemical on a small piece of inconspicuous fabric (a hem or seam) before treating the stain.

Treating vegetable stains

White cotton and linen. For a fresh stain, spread the fabric over a basin, spread with salt and pour boiling water through it. Wash and rinse. For a dried-in stain, stretch the fabric over a basin, dampen it and rub in oxalic acid with a bone or wooden spoon. (Do not use a metal spoon, which will be affected). Pour boiling water through, then neutralize the acid with a weak ammonia solution. Wash and rinse.

Above. Some of the chemicals used for stain removal. Always keep these separately from medicines, and out of reach of children.

Coloured cotton and linens, wool and silk. For fresh stains, spread the mark with glycerine and steep in a warm solution of borax. Wash and rinse. For old marks, sponge with sodium hydrosulphite bleach. Wash and rinse.

Synthetic fibres. For a fresh stain, apply glycerine and leave for a while. Dab with vinegar, then wash and rinse. For old marks, sponge with oxalic acid solution, neutralize with ammonia, then wash and rinse.

Treating protein stains

For fresh stains, the fabric should be steeped in cold water and salt (hot water sets the protein, and makes it much more difficult to remove). For old stains, soak the fabric in water with a biological washing powder, following the manufacturer's instructions. Really obstinate stains can be removed by steeping in a solution of hydrosulphite bleach.

Treating greasy stains

Scrape off any congealed grease with the back of a knife. Steep cotton and linens in hot water with detergent, then wash and rinse. Wash (without steeping) wools, silks and synthetic fabrics in warm water and detergent.

If the fabric is not washable, place the stain over clean blotting paper and iron on the wrong side to melt the grease. Move the blotting paper round as it absorbs the grease.

For more obstinate stains, place the fabric over blotting paper or a cotton pad, and apply carbon tetrachloride with cotton wool. Rub gently from the outside towards the middle of the stain until it is driven through.

Treating paint stains

To remove oil paint, put the stain over blotting

paper and sponge with a rag soaked with turpentine. Wash and rinse.

For cellulose paint and nail varnish, sponge with acetone or amyl acetate on cotton wool. Wash and rinse.

For fresh emulsion paint marks, soak in cold water and wash. With old marks, the fabric should be steeped in methylated spirit first.

Ink

One of the best ways of removing ballpoint ink is to sponge the mark with methylated spirit and rinse well.

Ordinary ink can usually be removed from fabric with detergent if treated quickly enough. Alternatively, steep the fabric in milk first and then wash. To remove ink from carpets, apply milk to the stain, leave for a few minutes and then rinse the carpet with a very weak solution of ammonia and water. A solution of water and vinegar can be used to treat ink marks on wood.

Scorch

Light marks can often be removed by soaking the fabric immediately in cold milk. Alternatively, soak cottons and linens in soap and hot water, and sponge other fabrics with diluted hydrosulphite bleach.

To treat unwashable materials, sponge with a solution of borax in hot water.

Bad marks, which have not damaged the fibres, can be treated with a paste made from borax and glycerine. Spread this thickly over the mark, leave overnight, then rinse and wash.

Very bad burns which have damaged the fibres of the fabric cannot be treated chemically, and usually have to be darned or patched.

Perspiration

If the fabric is washable, soak it in water with a biological washing powder. For unwashable fabric, sponge with methylated spirit or diluted vinegar.

DATA SHEET

Adhesives

This DATA SHEET is a valuable guide for the do-it-yourselfer. It gives you the information that is difficult to obtain elsewhere— what types of adhesive there are (and their British trade names), how to treat materials before glueing and, in easy to follow form, what types of glue will stick different materials together.

TABLE 1
This is a list of the various types of adhesive. Use it in conjunction with the chart on these pages and HOME ENGINEER 59.

Group 1 : animal glues
Croid Universal, Pearl, Duroglue, Mendit, Stycco, Certofix

Group 2 : clear general purpose
Durofix, Bostik 1, Dunlop Clear, Evostik Clear, Uhu, Balsa wood cement, Polystyrene cements, Quickfix

Group 3 : contact adhesive
Clam 3, Durofast, Unistik, Bostik 3, Dunlop Thixofix, Evo-stik Impact, Tretobond 404

Group 4 : latex
Copydex, Jiffybind, Jiffytex, Clam 5, Dunlop Carpet & Fabric Adhesive, Surestick

Group 5 : pva
Evostik Wood Adhesive, Bondfast, Unibond, Bondcrete, Borden Wood Glue, Bostik Carpentry, Clam 7, Timbabond 606

Group 6 : urea formaldehyde
Aerolite, Cascamite

Group 7 : epoxy
Araldite, Dunlop Epoxy, Bostik 7, Borden Power Pack

Group 8 : casein
Casco

Group 9 : ceiling cement for polystyrene tiles
Borden Polystyrene, Bostik 12, Dunlop Ceiling, Unibond E.P.A., Tretobond 282, Clam 24, Evostik Ceiling

Group 10 : floor tile cement
Bostik 11, Dunlop Semstik, Dunlop Flooring, Evostik Floor

Group 11 : wall tile cement
Bostik 10, Clam 2 or Clam 143, Dunlop Wall Tile Cement

Group 12 : wall and ceiling paper
Polycell, Stix, Clam, Dextrine, Slipsure

Group 13 : product adhesives

Some products, such as mineral acoustic tiles and plastic plumbing require special adhesives— these are usually supplied by the product manufacturer.

TABLE 2
Pre-treatment of various materials
This list briefly describes the pre-treatment of various materials prior to glueing.

Aluminium. Degrease, abrade or etch with chromic acid. Wash in cold water.

Asbestos board. Abrade. Use two coats of adhesive for very porous asbestos.

Brass and Bronze. Degrease, abrade or etch with acid ferric chloride.

Chromium. Degrease, abrade or etch with hot dilute sulphuric acid.

Concrete. Abrade if smooth.

Copper. Degrease, abrade or etch with acid ferric chloride.

Magnesium. Degrease, abrade or chromate finish.

Melinex. Degrease, abrade or treat with concentrated sodium hydroxide solution.

Polythene. Degrease and oxidize in flame or chromic acid.

Rubber. Treat for 5 min. with concentrated sulphuric acid or nitric acid. Wash and dry.

Mild steel. Degrease and abrade or etch with dilute phosphoric acid. Wash the metal with cold water and allow it to dry.

Stainless steel. Degrease and abrade or etch with hydrogen peroxide/formaldehyde solution used with caution.

Tungsten carbide. Degrease or treat with concentrated sodium hydroxide.

Wood. Abrade and dry.

Warning : Some of the chemicals listed above are dangerous if used incorrectly. Do not attempt these jobs if you have never done them before.

	Acoustic tiles (not polystyrene)	Carpet (not foam backed)	Ceramic tiles (floor)
Acoustic tiles (not polystyrene)	3	—	11
Carpet (not foam backed)	—	4	3,4
Ceramic tiles (floor)	11	3,4	7,10
Ceramic tiles (wall)	11	3,4	7,11
Cork	3,4,5	4	3,13
Fabrics/cloth	4,1,5	4	11,13
Glass/china/pottery	3	—	7
Hardboard	1,3,5	4,13	3,7
Leather	1,3,5	4	3
Leathercloth	1,3,4	3,4	3
Metal	3,7	3	7
Paper/card	1,2,3,4,5,12	1,4	2,4,11,12
Plaster (dried)	3,10,11	4,3	10
Plasterboard	2,13	3,4	10
Plastics—soft	2,13	2,13	2,13
Plastics—hard	3	2,3	3
Plastic laminate	1,3,5,6,7	3	3,7
Plastic floor tiles	2,10	—	2,13
Expanded polystyrene	9	5	—
Rubber	3	3	3
Stone	3,6,7	4,3	10
Wood	1,4,5,6,8	3,4,5	10,11
Bricks/concrete	3,13	4,3	2,3,10

	Fabrics/cloth	Glass/china/pottery	Hardboard	Leather	Leathercloth	Metal	Paper/card	Plaster (dried)	Plasterboard	Plastics—soft	Plastics—hard	Plastic laminate	Plastic floor tiles	Expanded polystyrene	Rubber	Stone	Wood	Bricks/concrete
5	4,1,5	3	1,3,5	1,3,5	1,3,4	3,7	1,2,3,4,5,12	3,10,11	2,13	2,13	3	1,3,5,6,7	2,10	9	3	3,6,7	1,4,5,6,8	3,13
	4	—	4,13	4	3,4	3	1,4	4,3	3,4	2,13	2,3	3	—	5	3	4,3	3,4,5	4,3
3	11,13	7	3,7	3	3	7	2,4,11,12	10	10	2,13	3	3,7	2,13	—	3	10	10,11	2,3,10
3	11,13	7	3,7	3	3	7	2,4,11,12	11	11	2,13	3	3,7	2,13	9	3	11	10,11	2,3,11
5	4,5	2	1,3,5	1,2,3,4	1,2,3,4	3	1,2,4,5,12	3,4,5	3,5,10	2,13	2,3	1,3	2,10	9	3	2,3,11	1,3,5	2,3,13
5	1,4	1,2,8	1,3,5	1,4,8	1,3,4	2,3	4	1,4,5	1,5	2,13	3	3	2,4	4,5	3	10	1,3,4,5,8	4
	1,2,8	2,7	7	1,2,7,8	2	2,7	2	2,7	2,7	2,13	2	3,7	—	—	2	2,7	—	7
5	1,3,5	7	1,3,5,8	1,3,5,8	1,3,4,5	3,7	1,3,4,5,12	3	3	2,13	3	1,3,7	2,10 13	5	3	3,7	1,5	3,5
8,4	1,4,8	1,2,7,8	1,3,5,8	1,3,4,8	1,4	3	2,4	3,4	3	2,13	2,3	3	2	4	3	3	1,3,4,8	—
8,4	1,3,4	2	1,3,4,5	1,4	1,2,4	2	2,4	2,3,4	1,2,3	2,13	2,3	3	3	—	—	2	1,3,5	—
	2,3	2,7	3,7	3	2	3,7	2,3	3,7	3,7	2,13	3,7	3,7	2	—	3	3,7	3,7	7
,5,	4	2	1,3,4,5,12	2,4	2	2,3	1,5,12	1,4,12	1,4,5,12	2,13	2	3,4	2	5,12	3	2	3,5,12	12
5	1,4,5	2,7	3	3,4	2,3,4	3,7	1,4,12	5,7	5	2,12	3	3,7	10,13	9	3	—	5,7	10,11
0	5	2,7	3	3	1,2,3	3,7	1,4,5,12	5	3,5	2,13	3	3,7	2	9	3	3	5	11
3	2,13	2,13	2,13	2,13	2,13	2,13	2,13	2,13	2,13	2,13	2,13	2	2	—	2	2	2	—
8	3	2	3	2,3	2,3	3,7	2	3	3	2,13	2,7,13	3,7	2	—	3	3,7,13	3,7	—
8	3	3,7	1,3,7	3	3	3,7	3,4	3,7	3,7	2	3,7	3,7	2,3	5	3	3,7	3,7	—
0	2,4	—	2,10,13	2	3	2	2	10,13	2	2	2	2,3	—	—	2	11	10	10,13
	4,5	—	5	4	—	—	5,12	9	9	—	—	5	—	9	—	9	9	9
1	3	2	3	3	—	3	3	3	3	2	3	3	2	—	3,4	3	3	—
1	10	2,7	3,7	3	2	3,7	2	—	3	2	3,7,13	3,7	11	11	3	7,10,11	3,6,7	7
5	1,3,4,5,8	—	1,5	1,3,4,8	1,3,5	3,7	3,5,12	5,7	5	2	3,7	3,7	10	10	3	6,7	1,3,5,6,8	—
13	4	7	3,5	—	—	7	12	10,11	11	—	—	—	10,13	9	—	7	—	—

INDEX

DATA SHEET

25 more handy hints

Professional craftsmen use these time saving hints daily to achieve good results. They save money too by showing how everyday articles substitute for expensive tools.

General

1. Soak oilstones in a tray of light oil such as corn oil or sewing-machine oil before use, for best results. Worn or uneven oilstones can be resurfaced by grinding them on a sheet of glass covered in 80 grit silicon carbide powder mixed with water.

2. Loosen a door that sticks along the bottom edge by pinning a piece of coarse sandpaper to the floor and swinging the door back and forth over it.

3. Cylinders can be held steady by sitting them in a V-grooved block—easy to make with a circular saw; otherwise use a tenon saw, keeping the cuts as straight as possible to stop the cylinder from rocking.

4. To insert a screw in a position you can't reach with your fingers, stick it to the tip of the screwdriver with thick grease or, in the case of heavy screws, adhesive tape.

5. When drilling horizontally into any surface with a twist or masonry bit, put a large washer halfway along the shank of the bit. If it moves towards you as you drill, lift the drill slightly; if it moves towards the surface, lower the drill. When it stays still, the drill is horizontal.

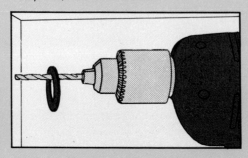

Carpentry

6. Large holes in timber are best filled with 'Dutch putty'—cellulose filler such as Polyfilla thinned with emulsion paint. This dries hard and much stronger than plain filler, and can easily be coloured with emulsion paint tinters.

7. When planing uneven timber, draw two or three pencil lines down the surface before you begin. These will then be planed off at the high spots first, revealing their location.

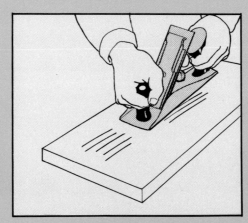

8. End grain planed without a shooting board tends to split. Avoid this by planing from the edges inwards; if you can't do this, bevel the edges all round first.

9. If you run out of G-cramps on a job, improvize with sections of car tyre inner tube used like giant rubber bands. Alternatively, use sash cord (but not nylon clothes line) with a piece of dowel passed through and turned to twist it tight.

10. A simple way of fixing a batten to a wall so that nothing shows is to drive a screw into a plug in the wall leaving (say) ½in. protruding. Drill a ½in. deep hole the width of the screw head in the back of the batten below the centre, and cut a slot the width of the screw shank upwards from this hole to the centre line. The batten can then be fitted over the screw head and tapped down.

11. Wood bits designed for handbraces can be converted to excellent power tool bits by cutting off the square top of the shank, filing three small flats around it to accept the three jaws of the chuck, and filing the screw thread off the tip (this step is important).

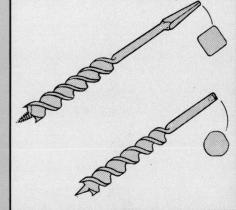

12. Butt joints in timber can be strengthened by driving slightly over-length nails right through and clenching (bending over) the protruding points. This must be done along the grain, so that the point sinks right in, and with the head of the nail supported, so that it is not driven back out of the wood. This creates a much stronger joint than a straight-through nail.

13. Always nail or screw through thin timber into thicker timber to give the fixings maximum holding power.